D&S
VOL. 31

COVERS ALL FIGHTER
AND RECONNAISSANCE VERSIONS

F-8 CRUSADER

in detail & scale

GW00683626

Bert Kinzey

TAB BOOKS Inc.
Blue Ridge Summit, PA

Airlife Publishing Ltd.
England

CONTRIBUTORS AND SOURCES:

Michael May	Roy Lock	Dave Ostrowski	Jim Galloway	Ray Wheeler
Dana Bell	Phillip Huston	Warren Munkasy	W. B. Baldwin	Clyde Mills
Lloyd Jones	Stephen Miller	Gustav Hebrok	Bill Wofford	Flightleader
Robert Davis	Bill Curry	Mick Roth	Don Harris	National Archives
John Ficklen	Chuck Stewart	Stan Piet	Robert Starnes	U.S. Navy
Ray Leader	Don Garrett	Bryan Wilburn	Jim Whitley	LTV Corporation
Ron Picciani	Ben Knowles	Bert Anido	Ed Husley	Centurion Enterprises

Photographs with no credit indicated were taken by the author.

FIRST EDITION
FIRST PRINTING

Published in United States by

TAB BOOKS Inc.
Blue Ridge Summit, PA 17294-0214

Library of Congress Cataloging
in Publication Data

Kinzey, Bert.
F-8 Crusader.

(Detail & Scale ; v. 31)
1. Crusader (Jet fighter plane) I. Title.
II. Title: F8 Crusader.
UG1242.F5K5275 1988   623.7464   88-28380
ISBN 0-8306-8541-3 (pbk.)

First published in Great Britain in 1988
by Airlife Publishing Ltd.
7 St. John's Hill, Shrewsbury, SY1 1JE

British Library Cataloging In
Publication Data

Kinzey, Bert, 1945-
F-8 Crusader.
I. Chance Vought F-8 aeroplanes, to 1987
I. Title II. Series
623.74′64

ISBN 1-85310-608-9

TAB BOOKS Inc. offers software for
sale. For information and a catalog,
please contact TAB Software Department,
Blue Ridge Summit, PA 17294-0850.

Questions regarding the content of this book
should be addressed to:

Reader Inquiry Branch
TAB BOOKS Inc.
Blue Ridge Summit, PA 17294-0214

Front cover: This beautiful painting by aviation artist John Ficklen depicts the F8U-2 Crusader from VF-84 flown by Bob Davis. Mr. Davis is now a pilot for Eastern Airlines, and has written a pilot's report for this book.

Rear cover: The instrument panel in one of the last operational RF-8Gs is shown from the right.

INTRODUCTION

The third F8U-1, 140446, is seen here on the deck of the USS FORRESTAL, CVA-59, during the carrier suitability evaluation on that carrier. Evaluations were also conducted on the USS BON HOMME RICHARD, CVA-31, of the smaller ESSEX class.   *(National Archives)*

If there was one thing you could count on when it came to carrier-based aviation, it was that any shipboard fighter designed by Chance Vought would have some unusual, if not radical, design feature. Prior to the 1950s, Chance Vought had established itself as one of the more successful producers of aircraft for the U.S. Navy, probably second only to Grumman, and their most successful product had been the famous F4U Corsair that had served well in both World War II and Korea. Many observers considered the F4U as the best propeller driven fighter of World War II, but it had some of those "unusual" features that caused some problems early on. In order to keep the landing gear as short and strong as possible, while allowing room for a propeller of large diameter, the Corsair featured an inverted gull wing. The cockpit was well aft, which made it difficult for a pilot to see where he was going on the ground or on a carrier. In the air the F4U was excellent. Coming aboard carriers, it left a lot to be desired. A small spoiler on the leading edge of the right wing, a redesigned canopy, and a higher seat were some of the fixes that eventually made the Corsair one of the best carrier-based, propeller-driven fighters ever designed. It established Chance Vought's reputation as a

successful aircraft manufacturer.

But the post-war years and the entry into the jet age were not as kind to the people at the Dallas-based company. Their first jet-powered design, the XF6U Pirate was not a success by any standards, with only thirty-three being produced. Some were fitted with afterburners, being the first Navy aircraft to have these new thrust augmentation devices. Then came the F7U Cutlass, which faired better than the Pirate, but it could not be truly judged a success. However, the Cutlass did maintain Chance Vought's reputation for radical features, since it did not look like anything else in the sky. It was a tailless design, having no horizontal tail plane and two vertical fins mounted on the trailing edge of the wing. It was the first aircraft designed from the start with afterburners, but even these provided less than satisfactory performance.

Keeping the wing at high angles of attack for take-offs and landings was a problem in the early years of jet aircraft, particularly when it came to operating from carriers. To solve this problem, the Cutlass had an extremely long nose gear strut that wound up being a major problem. It held the nose very high, and to provide the best

3

The most unusual feature of the Crusader's design was a two-position wing. It is shown here in the raised position. When the wing was in this position, the leading edge droops, the flaps, and the ailerons were automatically placed in a lowered position.

(U.S. Navy)

visibility over it, the cockpit was placed as far forward as possible--right above the strut. There is more than one incident recorded where the strut collapsed and went up through the cockpit killing the pilot where he sat, or causing the ejection seat to fire, also killing the pilot in the process. The Cutlass proved conclusively that long landing gear struts and carrier operations just don't mix, and like the early Corsairs, the Cutlass had a lot of problems operating around carriers.

Then came the Crusader. While not as radical as the Cutlass, the design of the F8U departed significantly from the standard. Ever since the monoplane had replaced the biplane as the primary fighter design two decades earlier, fighters were almost always fitted with mid or low-mounted wings. But the Crusader had a high-mounted wing that was the largest on any fighter up until that time. Today, a number of fighters from the F-15 to the MiG-25 have high-mounted wings, but in the mid-1950s it was almost unique. Additionally, the leading edge of the wing could be raised or lowered in flight so as to change its angle of attack without changing the pitch attitude of the entire aircraft. This feature, combined with a cockpit well forward on the fuselage, provided the pilot an excellent view during landings and take-offs, and permitted the necessary slow flying speeds required for carrier operations. But the Crusader also incorporated sound design features and the latest advances in construction methods, use of metals, and a good engine. The result

was a design that combined new features with state-of-the-art technology and proven concepts.

The designers and engineers at Chance Vought were convinced that the Crusader would be a success, and the aircraft did not let them down. It became the first aircraft to exceed Mach 1 during its very first flight. It was the first to set a world speed record in excess of 1000 miles per hour. It won both the Thompson and Collier Trophies, and racked up a number of other outstanding firsts. It became the fastest single-engined carrier-based fighter ever built, and it still holds that distinction today. F-8s performed well in the skies over Vietnam, not only killing MiGs, but as a fighter-bomber as well.

On the pages that follow is a close-up look at what has to be one of the most important aircraft designs in history. Following a brief historical summary and a pilot's report is a look at each version of the Crusader. All of the major details, from cockpits to landing gear, and control surfaces to armament and external stores are illustrated with scores of photographs, many of which were taken specifically for this publication. Detailed drawings provide a further look at many features. A five-view drawing, done specifically for this publication by Dana Bell, is also included. Our Modeler's Section contains a summary of all of the currently available kits from the oldest to the newly-released Monogram model, and reviews those that are presently available. A decal listing is also provided.

The clean, straight-forward lines of the Crusader are evident in this view of one of the prototypes. Visible are the extended boarding step and fold-down hand holds/steps, the partially open speed brake, the original spoked wheels, and the instrumentation probe on the nose.
(National Archives)

In The Beginning

With the success of the F4U Corsair and a large number of orders for that aircraft, Chance Vought had prospered during World War II and for several years thereafter. Corsairs were still flying in considerable numbers during the Korean War, but time was running out. Chance Vought, then a member of the United Aircraft Corporation, had its back against the wall. Its three designs since the Corsair had not faired as well. The XF5U Flying Flapjack was never put into production. Their first jet, the F6U Pirate, was also unsuccessful, with only a handful being built. The F7U Cutlass was only moderately successful and was not produced in large enough numbers to keep the company alive. It was difficult to fly from carriers, and its performance was not promising. The future for the Cutlass was not bright nor lengthy, and Chance Vought realized that.

In September 1952, the Navy Bureau of Aeronautics issued a requirement for a new supersonic, carrier-based, air superiority fighter. Chance Vought had only eight months to come up with a proposal, so Russ Clark and his design team had a lot of work to do in a short time. They designed a fighter with a high-mounted wing that was unheard of at that time. In keeping with the company's tradition of radical design features, the wing was hinged to move seven degrees in incidence, and was controlled hydraulically. Devices called droops were located along the entire span of the leading edge, and the ailerons and small flaps were located inboard of the wing fold on the trailing edge. All of this was incorporated into the wing design in order to give the supersonic aircraft good handling and flight characteristics required at slow carrier landing speeds. Additionally, the wing had a forty-two-degree sweep at quarter chord and a five degree

anhedral. There were no spoilers on the wing, meaning that the ailerons provided all roll control. The all-flying horizontal stabilizers were mid-mounted on the aft fuselage, and operated in unison to provide pitch control. They did not work in opposite directions to provide roll control. The leading edge had a saw tooth at the wing fold line--the first designed into any aircraft from the beginning. The purpose of the saw tooth was to minimize a tendency to pitch up at high speed and decrease instability when approaching stall speeds. The wing area was 350 square feet, the largest on any jet fighter at that time.

The fuselage followed the area rule design principle without the noticeable wasp waist or coke bottle shape that was characteristic of other fighters developed during this same time period. The cockpit was located as far forward as possible to provide good forward and lateral visibility.

Armament consisted of four Colt 20mm cannon located in the forward fuselage, and thirty-two 2.75-inch rockets in a "drawer" mounted just forward of the main gear in the lower fuselage.

Because of the high wing, the landing gear was mounted on the fuselage, was short, and had the strength required for carrier operations. Chance Vought had obviously learned its lessons with the long-legged Cutlass which had wing-mounted main gear and a two-story nose gear. The latest construction techniques would be used for the Crusader, and extensive amounts of magnesium and titanium were included in the design.

Pratt & Whitney was also a member of United Aircraft, and Chance Vought selected the P&W J57 engine to power its fighter. It promised excellent performance, and was used in more jet aircraft than any other engine developed during that time frame. An internal fuel load of 1,165

This interesting shot shows F8U-1, 140446, being prepared for a launch from a land catapult. Both the launch bridle and the holdback cable are clearly visible. (National Archives)

gallons was provided in wing and fuselage tanks.

The designers at Chance Vought believed that they had a winner, and their confidence was justified in May 1953 when their design was chosen over seven others for further development. An order was placed for three prototype XF8U-1s on June 29, 1953, but this was subsequently changed to only two aircraft. Early production F8U-1s were used for further testing and evaluation. Chance Vought broke away from United Aircraft and became independent, remaining so until becoming a part of Ling-Temco-Vought in 1963.

On March 25, 1955, John Konrad took the first prototype up for its maiden flight and exceeded Mach 1, making the Crusader the first aircraft ever to do so on its first flight. This was the first of many "firsts" that would be achieved by the F-8 over the next few years.

An Unqualified Success

The importance of the Crusader to the Navy cannot be overstated. In 1955 the Navy was spending a great deal of money modernizing its Essex class carriers with angle decks. Construction of the first large-deck supercarriers in the Forrestal class was well underway. But carrier-based fighters were falling far behind their land-based counterparts in the Air Force when it came to almost every performance category. Many military and civilian leaders, especially Air Force generals, were trying to write off Naval fighters and the aircraft carrier completely. They were competing for limited funds, and they felt that money could be better spent on the B-36 and the better-performing land-based fighters. But the Crusader was not only to prove these generals wrong, it made them sit up and take notice. It was the beginning of a trend

where a number of Naval aircraft not only equalled, but exceeded the Air Force's designs. The next fighter that the Navy would develop, the F-4 Phantom, would not only be better than anything the Air Force had, it would be purchased by the Air Force, and it would become their mainstay for many years. Although the Crusader itself would never fly in Air Force colors, the A-7 Corsair II, which was based on the Crusader's design, would find its way into Air Force squadrons.

More than any other factors, the success of the Crusader and the improvements to carrier designs saved tail hook aviation in the U.S. Navy. From the first flight of the XF8U-1, it became clear that carrier-based fighters could be the equal to, and even better than, land-based fighters. A good comparison can be made between the Crusader and the Air Force's F-100 that was developed at the same time and had the same engine. The Crusader had superior speed at all altitudes, better trans-sonic acceleration, better rate of climb, better roll rate and turn rate, more range, and better slow speed characteristics. Reports from the Soviet Union indicated that they considered the Crusader the best Western fighter. Obviously, there were people on this side of the Iron Curtain that agreed. The Crusader won the Collier Trophy for design and development, the Thompson Trophy for its record-setting speed, and the first ever Bureau of Aeronautics Certificate of Merit.

Firsts and More Firsts

Being the first aircraft to exceed Mach 1 during its maiden flight was only the beginning for the Crusader when it came to accomplishing aviation "firsts." PROJECT ONE GRAND was flown on August 21, 1956, by

CDR. R. W. "Duke" Windsor. It was an attempt by the Navy to set the first official speed record in excess of 1000 miles per hour. The flight was flown at an altitude of 40,000 feet over the fifteen-kilometer course at the Naval Ordnance Test Station located at China Lake, California. It is also important to note that the Navy did not modify the aircraft, but used a production F8U-1 with full cannon armament and dummy ammunition. The speed of 1015.428 miles per hour not only set the first speed record in excess of 1000 miles per hour, but because a standard production aircraft was used, the Crusader also became the first operationally equipped jet fighter to fly faster than 1000 miles per hour. This exceeded the previous record of 822 miles per hour, set by an F-100, by a considerable margin. It was for this record-setting flight that the Crusader captured the Thompson Trophy.

On June 6, 1957, two Crusaders piloted by CAPT G. Robert Dose and LCDR Paul Miller, Jr., took off from the USS Bon Homme Richard, CVA-31, as the carrier steamed in the Pacific off the California coast. The two Crusaders were assigned to VF-32, and flew in the company of two A3D Skywarriors that also launched from the carrier. The four aircraft headed east across the United States and finally recovered aboard the USS Saratoga, CVA-60, in the Atlantic. This was the first carrier-to-carrier transcontinental flight, and was completed by the F8Us in three hours and twenty-eight minutes. This set an unofficial cross-country speed record. The A3Ds took four hours and one minute. President Eisenhower was aboard the Saratoga to witness the event thirteen years to the day after he had commanded the Allied landings at Normandy.

The following month, PROJECT BULLET was flown to make the cross-country record official. On July 16, 1957, an F8U-1P, 144608, piloted by Marine Major John H. Glenn, Jr., took off from Los Alamitos, California, and flew to Floyd Bennett Field, New York, in three hours, twenty-two minutes, and 50.05 seconds. Average speed for the trip was 723.517 miles per hour, making this the first upper atmosphere supersonic flight from the west coast to the east coast. Glenn, later one of the original seven Mercury astronauts, the first American to orbit the earth, and a U.S. Senator from Ohio, kept his cameras rolling, making a continuous film strip of the United States beneath his aircraft. He completed three in-flight refuelings during the trip, and received the Distinguished Flying Cross for his achievement.

As originally planned, PROJECT BULLET was to be flown by two aircraft, but the second, an F8U-1, piloted by LT Charles Demmler, received damage to its refueling probe over Albuquerque, New Mexico, and had to land.

OPERATION PIPELINE was completed by four F8U Crusaders and four F3H Demons on May 17, 1958. This was a practical demonstration to show the speed with

GENERAL ARRANGEMENT

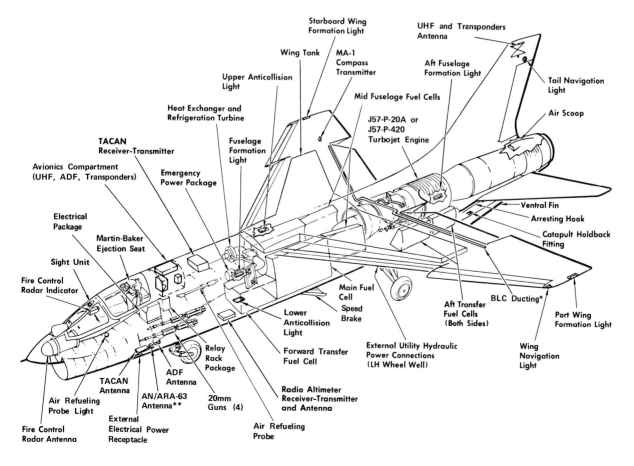

which carrier aircraft could be delivered from the east coast to the Sixth Fleet operating in the Mediterranean Sea. It was the first nonstop trans-Atlantic crossing by jet aircraft to a carrier in the Mediterranean.

On January 17, 1962, CDR George Talley, flying a Crusader from VF-62, made the first arrested landing on the first nuclear powered aircraft carrier, the USS Enterprise, CVA(N)-65. This marked the beginning of the carrier's flight operations. VF-62's Crusaders then became the first aircraft to make catapult launches and then recover aboard Enterprise. A few days later, on January 23, OPERATION PINE NEEDLE was completed when the last of eighteen Crusaders from Marine squadron VMF (AW)-451 arrived at Atsugi, Japan, from MCAS El Toro. This was the first trans-Pacific flight by a Marine Corps jet fighter squadron, and was led by LTC Charles E. Crew, commanding officer of the squadron.

The first fully automatic carrier landings with production equipment were made on June 13, 1963, by LCDR R. K. Billings and LCDR R.S. Chew, Jr., flying an F-4A and F-8D respectively. The traps were made aboard the USS Midway, CVA-41, operating off the California coast, and both the flight controls and throttles were operated automatically by signals from the ship. Although similar landings had been made before with test aircraft, this accomplishment with production aircraft highlighted almost ten years of research and development.

Perhaps the most unusual first accomplished by the Crusader, and a capability its designers never envisioned, was its ability to fly with its wings folded. This was made possible by the fact that enough lift was provided by the wing's center section alone, and because the flaps and ailerons were both inboard of the wing fold. If the ailerons had been outboard of the wing fold, such flight would not have been possible regardless of how much lift was generated by the wing's center section. There are no less than seven separate recorded incidents where an F-8 flew with its wings in the folded position, none of which were made deliberately. The first of these took place at Capodichino Airport, Naples, Italy, on August 2,

1960. LT Jack Barnes, of VF-11, inadvertently took off with the wings folded. When he noticed the problem, he climbed to 5000 feet, dumped his fuel, and safely made a "hot" landing. The entire flight took about twenty-four minutes. On two occasions, pilots who had taken off with the wings folded were able to climb to altitude, extend first one wing and then the other. This would seem to be even more dangerous than flying with both wings folded, since the center of lift would be altered considerably with one wing extended and one folded. However, both pilots accomplished the maneuver successfully, then continued their flights in a routine manner.

It did not require a clean aircraft to fly the Crusader with the wings folded. There were two incidents where flights were made with external stores attached to the aircraft. In August 1966, a Marine Corps Crusader from VMF (AW)-235 took off from Da Nang with two 1000-pound bombs for a night strike. Once the pilot noticed the problem, he landed the aircraft safely, although the landing gear collapsed because of the heavy weight and "hot" landing. The second "loaded" flight with the wings folded also happened at Da Nang and involved another VMF (AW)-235 aircraft. On this occasion the Crusader was loaded with Zuni rockets and a 1000-pound bomb load. After the pilot jettisoned these in the Gulf of Tonkin, he returned and landed safely at Da Nang.

Crusader Variants

Although the Crusader was involved in many firsts, its primary reason for existing was to serve the Navy as a carrier-based fighter aircraft. Following the two prototypes, the first production version was the F8U-1, which was later designated F-8A. This was followed by four more fighter versions and one photo-reconnaissance version. Except for the F-8A, each of these variants went through a remanufacture program costing $200 million and involving 448 aircraft. This remanufacturing program extended the service life of the aircraft by strengthening and reinforcing the airframe and landing gear. It also upgraded the capabilities to varying extents depending

*With shock diamonds visible in its exhaust flame, this F8U-1, later redesignated the F-8A, streaks across the sky. The aircraft belongs to the Naval Air Test Center, as indicated by the **NATC** on its tail.*   *(National Archives)*

on the model involved. Each variant and its remanufactured version is covered in separate sections beginning on page 17.

In any reference on the Crusader, mention must be made concerning the original designations and the new DOD designations that replaced them in 1962. For the most part we are using the new designations in this book except when it seems more appropriate to use the original ones. The following table shows the original Navy designations, the new DOD designations, and the designation for the corresponding remanufactured versions.

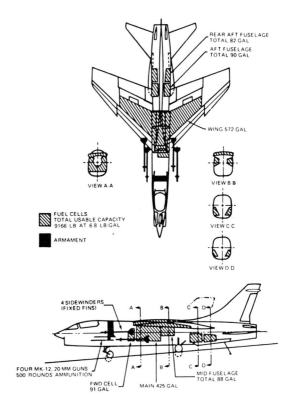

CRUSADER DESIGNATIONS

ORIGINAL DESIGNATION	1962 DOD DESIGNATION	REMANUFACTURED DESIGNATION	
XF8U-1	-	-	
F8U-1	F-8A	F-8M*	(0)
F8U-1E	F-8B	F-8L	(63)
F8U-2	F-8C	F-8K	(87)
F8U-2N	F-8D	F-8H	(89)
F8U-2NE	F-8E	F-8J	(136)
F8U-1P	RF-8A	RF-8G	(73)
F8U-1T	TF-8A	-	

* The F-8M remanufacturing program was not implemented. Numbers in ( ) show the number of aircraft remanufactured.

This drawing shows armament and fuel tank locations for F-8D and F-8E aircraft. (U.S. Navy)

MAJOR CHARACTERISTICS AND DIFFERENCES TABLE FOR F-8 CRUSADER VARIANTS AS ORIGINALLY MANUFACTURED

CHARACTERISTIC	F-8A	F-8C	F-8D	F-8E	RF-8A
Engine (All Pratt & Whitney)	J57-P-4	J57-P-16	J57-P-20	J57-P-20	J57-P-4
Length	250"	270"	269.52"	269.52"	250"
Diameter	41"	40.44"	40.44"	40.44"	41"
Thrust					
Military + Afterburner	16,000 lbs.	16,900 lbs.	18,000 lbs.	18,000 lbs.	16,000 lbs.
Military	10,200 lbs.	10,700 lbs.	10,700 lbs.	10,700 lbs.	10,200 lbs.
Normal	8,700 lbs.	9,150 lbs.	9,150 lbs.	9,150 lbs.	8,700 lbs.
Weights					
Empty	15,513 lbs.	16,483 lbs.	17,541 lbs.	17,836 lbs.	16,796 lbs.
Basic	16,171 lbs.	17,673 lbs.	18,432 lbs.	18,432 lbs.	17,564 lbs.
Design	21,442 lbs.	23,192 lbs.	26,000 lbs.	26,000 lbs.	24,000 lbs.
Combat	20,995 lbs.	24,475 lbs.	25,098 lbs.	30,232 lbs.	23,752 lbs.
Max T.O. Field	27,500 lbs.	27,938 lbs.	29,500 lbs.	34,100 lbs.	27,822 lbs.
Max T.O. Catapult	27,500 lbs.	27,938 lbs.	29,500 lbs.	34,100 lbs.	27,822 lbs.
Max Landing Field	23,500 lbs.	23,500 lbs.	26,000 lbs.	26,000 lbs.	23,500 lbs.
Max Landing Arrested	20,000 lbs.	22,000 lbs.	22,000 lbs.	22,000 lbs.	20,000 lbs.
Internal Fuel Capacity	1,273 gal.	1,273 gal.	1,348 gal.	1,348 gal.	1,497 gal.
Radar/Gunsight	AN/APG-30A	AN/APS-67	AN/APQ-83	AN/APQ-94	NONE
Armament					
Mark 12 20mm Cannon (Rounds)	4 (500)	4 (500)	4 (500)	4 (500)	NONE
2.75 inch FFAR Rockets	32	32	NONE	NONE	NONE
AIM-9 Sidewinder Missiles	2	2	4	4	NONE
External Stores on Wings	NONE	NONE	NONE	YES	NONE
Afterburner Cooling Scoops	NO	YES	YES	YES	NO
Ventral Fins	NO	YES	YES	YES	NO
First Flight	March 1955	August 1958	February 1960	September 1961	January 1957
First Service Use	March 1957	February 1959	October 1960	Unknown	November 1957

NOTES: F-8B characteristics are the same as for the F-8A except that the F-8B had the AN/APS-67 radar.
Combat weights are for maximum ordnance loading to include wing stores if applicable.
Source: Standard Aircraft Characteristics, U.S. Navy.

TF-8A DUAL COCKPIT ARRANGEMENT

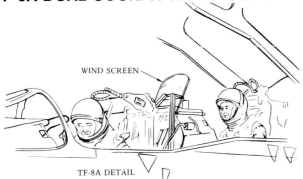

WIND SCREEN

TF-8A DETAIL

Drawing Courtesy of Vought Aeronautics

After serving as the prototype for the F-8E, 143710, which was originally an F-8A, became the only two-seat trainer version of the Crusader. It was referred to as the "Two-sader" and "Crew-sader," and after serving with NASA, was recalled to help Philippine pilots learn to fly the F-8. However, it was lost in a crash on July 28, 1978.

(Flightleader)

Operational History

VF-32 was the first unit to become operational with the Crusader and deploy aboard a carrier. They had little time to get to know their new fighter when the crisis in Lebanon began in the summer of 1958. VF-32 was embarked aboard the USS Saratoga, CVA-60, and was part of the show of force by the United States. Crusaders flew 533 hours in July and 762 in August. VMF-333, embarked in the USS Forrestal, CVA-59, relieved VF-32 in August.

The next big event for the Crusader was the Cuban Missile Crisis in 1962. RF-8As, escorted by fighter versions of the Crusader, were among several types of reconnaissance aircraft that took photographs over the island of Cuba to verify the presence and removal of Soviet missiles from that island nation only ninety miles from American soil.

By the time the Pueblo Crisis occurred in June 1968, early models of the Crusader had been relegated to the reserves, and President Johnson called up six reserve Navy fighter and attack squadrons. VF-703 at Dallas, VF-661 from NAS Andrews, and VF-931 from NAS Willow Grove, each flying Crusaders, answered the call-up which lasted until November 1968. By then the "big show" was well underway in a place most Americans had pre-viously never heard of--Vietnam.

By March 1967, the Crusader was a proven aircraft with ten years of service, 1,500,000 flying hours, and 250,000 arrested landings. It had equipped thirty active Navy and Marine squadrons and twenty reserve squadrons. Almost two years had elapsed since its first use in Vietnam which occurred on May 25, 1965. On that date VF-162, flying from the USS Oriskany, CVA-34, participated in the attack against Mui Song. The first MiG kill scored by a Crusader during the war in Vietnam was made by CDR Harold Marr, when he shot down a MiG-17 northeast of Haiphong. Eighteen more confirmed kills would be made before the Crusader flew its last mission.

It was the MiG kills that would be the most publicized aspect of the Crusader's exploits in Southeast Asia, but there was a lot more to it than that. Navy F-8s were embarked on Essex class carriers (plus one cruise aboard the USS Coral Sea, CVA-43, of the Midway class), while the Marines flew F-8s from land bases in South Vietnam. One Marine squadron, VMF-212, operated from the USS Oriskany during 1965. RF-8s were provided on a continuing basis by VFP-63 to perform the photographic reconnaissance mission. With a lack of serious air opposition throughout most of the war, Crusaders were often loaded with bombs, rockets, and guided missiles to attack ground targets. Fighter pilots, who were used to yanking and banking with the F-8's superior dogfighting wing, were not ecstatic about having their aircraft turned into a fighter-bomber. It was not the primary mission that they were trained for, nor the one the aircraft was designed for. While the Crusader did a respectable job of attacking ground targets, using its gunsight to deliver the ordnance, it was not in the same class with the Air Force versions of the F-4 or the F-105 that were designed with the delivery systems and ordnance-carrying capability necessary for a true fighter-bomber. Beginning on page 56 is a look at the armament carried by the fighter versions of the Crusader.

One of the interesting "field fixes" made to the Crusader during the war was the addition of switches that allowed the firing of only two guns at a time. The F-8's four 20mm cannon were installed with the idea of shooting down aircraft. The rapid rate of fire necessary to successfully hit and destroy an aerial target meant that the 500 rounds of ammunition were expended very quickly--in about ten seconds. During strafing attacks, and in particular during RESCAP missions, it was more important to be able to fire over longer periods of time. Therefore, switches were installed in some aircraft to allow them to fire the top two, bottom two, or all four guns at once. This meant that the Crusader could fly twice as many passes for twice the time covering a downed pilot. Two guns provided plenty of firepower for this mission.

Although killing MiGs receives the glamour and the press, it was something that didn't happen all that often in Vietnam. Relative to the time spent flying sorties against ground targets, escort, and various other missions, the time spent actually engaging enemy aircraft was minuscule. Between June 12, 1966, when the first MiG kill was scored by a Crusader, until April 22, 1972, which was the date of the last, only nineteen MiGs were confirmed destroyed by F-8s. Only one victory was scored with guns alone. In between, countless sorties were flown without even seeing the enemy in the air. But when the time came to mix it up, the Crusader proved itself a real champion. More kills were scored by Phantoms, but the F-4 was used in far greater numbers. The Crusader compiled the highest kill ratio of any fighter in the war. Its wing was considered to be the best dogfighting wing on any American fighter, and it was more able to hassle with the lighter MiGs than the F-4. Until the Air Force introduced the F-4E, the Phantoms did not have internal cannon armament, but the Crusader did, and this was a distinct advantage when fighting in close. Further, the Crusader could fire its guns from any angle, including a head-on pass. But it was the Sidewinder that was used most often by Crusader pilots to score their kills. Sidewinders were used in combination with guns on a number of occasions, and in one case, a kill was scored using guns and Zuni rockets. Undoubtedly the most unusual "kill" was also the last, and the only one made by an F-8J. LT Gerald Tucker, of VF-211 and the USS Hancock, CVA-19, was closing on a MiG-17 when the enemy pilot ejected before a shot was fired! It can be debated whether this should be a confirmed "kill," but the MiG was destroyed when it impacted the ground without its pilot, and destroying the MiG was what it was all about.

The primary purpose of this publication is to illustrate the details of the various versions of the F-8, not to provide a lengthy documentary on its history, even that of killing MiGs. For the reader interested in further information on this aspect of the Crusader's service, Detail & Scale recommends Barrett Tillman's excellent book, MiG Master: The Story of the F-8 Crusader, published by The Nautical & Aviation Publishing Company of America, 8 Randall Street, Annapolis, Maryland 21401. For several reasons, we believe it to be Tillman's best book of the several he has written.

The International Scene

When the French Navy needed a fighter for its two aircraft carriers, Foch and Clemenceau, the Crusader seemed to be the ideal choice. The only problem was that the French carriers were even smaller than the U.S. Navy's Essex class, so ways had to be found to permit the French Crusaders to operate at even slower approach speeds. The result was the F-8E (FN), which was basically an F-8E with some changes made for the French. These included boundary layer control, which used air from the engine's high-pressure compressor, and forced it through nozzles located on top of the wing. The blown air passed over the flaps and "tricked" the wing and flaps into thinking the wing was flying faster than it actually was. Double-hinged leading edge droops replaced the single-hinged units used on the U.S. Navy's aircraft. With these two changes to the wing, French Crusaders could fly their approaches at ninety knots! A larger horizontal tail for better control at slower speeds was also fitted. Inside the airframe were electronics to allow an interface with the Matra R 530 missile, and a titanium leading edge was added to the horizontal stabilizers to resist the blast of the Matra missiles. The French version was fitted with the J57-P-20A engine.

The prototype for the F-8E (FN) was F-8D, 147036, and it made its first flight on February 26, 1964. But it crashed the following April, so further testing was done on production French aircraft. Initial carrier tests were flown aboard the USS Shangri-La, CVA-38, by both French and U.S. pilots, who then moved to the Clemenceau for evaluation. In October 1964, Flottile 12F became the first French squadron to receive the Crusader, and this was followed by Flottile 14F. Each had twelve aircraft, and employed them only in the air-to-air role, not for ground attack. The total French order was for thirty-six aircraft, and at one time, they operated six single-seat trainers of F-8A standards for training purposes. The last French Crusader built was also the last of any Crusader built new, and was completed in January 1965. But the high-lift devices employed by the French: the double-

The first foreign user of the Crusader was the French Navy. The F-8E (FN) had the double hinge line on the leading edge droops that would later be used on the F-8J.
(Flightleader)

The second and only other foreign user of the Crusader was the Philippine Air Force. They received thirty-five former F-8Hs in 1977, which were designated F-8Ps.
(Huston)

hinged, double-segmented droops, the boundary layer control, and the larger horizontal stabilizer were all carried forward to the F-8E remanufacturing program that resulted in the F-8J.

The second foreign nation to purchase the Crusader was the Philippines, who obtained thirty-five former F-8Hs in 1977 at a cost of just under twelve million dollars. The aircraft were in storage at Davis-Monthan at that time. Twenty-five were overhauled at Vought for an additional twenty-three million dollars, while the other ten were used for spares. With no aircraft carriers in their Navy, the Filipinos used their F-8P Crusaders from land bases only.

The Super Crusader

Even a summary of the Crusader's history would not be complete without the mention of the XF8U-3 Crusader III which evolved from the basic Crusader design. However, similarity was actually rather superficial, with more differences existing than commonalities. Fitted with a J75 engine, the Crusader III was a powerful aircraft, and plans were included for a throttleable rocket engine, although it was never fitted. Original blueprints of the aircraft show an intake like that on the standard Crusaders, but the actual prototype was fitted with a large intake that slanted forward to the lip. A radar that was located in a large radome above the intake provided a true all-weather capability and guided three AIM-7 Sparrow missiles housed in semi-recessed bays under the fuselage. There was no gun armament, but provisions were made for four wing pylons, although they were never fitted. The nose wheel was offset to the right, and there were two hinged stabilizing fins attached to the aft fuselage.

The first flight of the three flying prototypes was made by John Konrad on June 2, 1958. During testing, a speed

The F8U-3 Crusader III was an outstanding aircraft, but lost out in a competition with the McDonnell Phantom. While sharing similarities with the basic F-8 design, it was really a new aircraft with all-weather capability.

(U.S. Navy via Jones)

This photograph shows the Crusader III in flight with its ventral fins in the lowered "flying" position. They rotated to a horizontal position for ground operations, as seen in the photograph at left. (U.S. Navy via Jones)

of Mach 2.6 was reached, and the aircraft had the potential for more. In almost all respects it seemed to be an outstanding aircraft, but it was in competition with the F4H Phantom II. The F4H had two seats and two engines, and this seemed to be the direction the Navy wanted to go. Further, as time proved so well, the Phantom was also a superior aircraft, so the XF8U-3 lost out to a design that would have beaten out just about any other aircraft, not just the Crusader III. The XF8U-3 has been called "the best airplane ever cancelled," and was turned over to NASA for further testing.

A Number of Lasts

Previously we mentioned some of the "firsts" accomplished by the Crusader early in its service life. It also recorded a number of "lasts." It was the last single-seat, single-engine fighter in Navy service. It was the last Navy fighter designed with its air intake in the nose. (The A-7 is considered by the Navy to be an attack aircraft, not a fighter.) It was the last fighter to be deployed aboard the Essex class carriers, and when the last Essex class carrier was retired from fleet service in 1976, the fighter versions of the Crusader were likewise retired. It was the last aircraft initially designed as a "day" fighter with no all-weather or night capability, although a limited capability was later added. The RF-8G was the last dedicated photo-reconnaissance asset in the Navy, the last of which was retired from Naval Reserve service in March 1987. It was the last fighter built by Vought, and with its end, and the present phasing out of the A-7 Corsair II, Vought, long a builder of aircraft for the Navy, no longer is producing new aircraft. When the Phantom was introduced without gun armament, the Crusader was also called "the last of the gunfighters," but common sense has made this expression obsolete as guns were put back in fighters after the lessons were learned in Vietnam. But there will also be a close-knit band of pilots who will tell you, "When you are out of Crusaders, you are out of fighters!"

PILOT'S REPORT

VF-84 was the first squadron to receive the F-8C version of the Crusader. Here, two of the squadron's aircraft are being moved to position on the numbers one and two catapults on the USS INDEPENDENCE, CVA-62, during the F-8C's first deployment. *(U.S. Navy via Davis)*

Bob Davis now flies for Eastern Air Lines, but he was once a Crusader pilot with time in all versions. He was a member of VF-84 when they took the F8U-2 on its first deployment aboard the USS Independence (CVA-62). John Ficklen's beautiful painting that appears on the cover of this book depicts the Crusader flown by LT Bob Davis during that time. Bob also served as an instructor pilot with VF-174, the east coast Crusader training squadron. Detail & Scale asked him to think back about a quarter of a century, and recall some of his more memorable moments with the aircraft. The following is what Bob had to say.

VF-84 was the first squadron to receive the F8U-2 (F-8C) version of the Crusader. They operated it from 1959 to 1964 as a part of Air Group 7 aboard the USS Independence, CVA-62, and were home based at NAS Oceana. The squadron made four cruises to the Mediterranean, provided fighter cover for the photo aircraft just after the ill-fated Bay of Pigs invasion, and was part of the Cuban Blockade from its beginning until a standdown was declared. Numerous other shorter deployments were also made. VF-84 twice received the coveted Atlantic Fleet "E" (Excellence) award for being the top day fighter squadron. At the time VF-84 received the F8U-2, it was the fastest and best performing carrier-based day fighter in the world. Engine thrust was significantly increased over earlier models, and ventral fins were added to the lower aft fuselage for stability above 1.5 Mach.

The primary role of the Crusader was supremacy in aerial combat, better known as dogfighting. With its tremendous power and maneuverability, the F8U-2 was not only the the best carrier-based day fighter of its time, whatever was second best wasn't even close! This is not meant to put down the other carrier-based fighter of that era, the F-4B Phantom. The F-4B had a better thrust-to-weight ratio than the F8U, but it was not designed or flown as a close-combat, pure dogfighting airplane.

The F8U-2 was the last of the pure "day" fighters. It was the third in a line of five fighter versions of the Crusader built for the Navy. The last two versions, the F8U-2N and F8U-2NE, were designated "night" or "all weather" models. One unarmed photo version of the aircraft was also produced, this being the F8U-1P. The fighter versions had four 20mm cannon, and, depending on aircraft model, two or four Sidewinder air-to-air missiles could be carried. The Sidewinders of that time required a "tail shot" at the enemy aircraft, so maneuvering for the kill was the name of the game. That was the difference between the Crusader pilot and the F-4B "shoot in the dark" interceptor Phantom drivers with their radar guided Sparrow missiles. Much of this would change in Vietnam, but in the early 1960s, that was the difference between the two aircraft and the pilots that flew them.

Aside from its obvious size, the single most impressive thing about the Crusader was the engine thrust. It could operate in sustained high G turns and in the vertical. It was not docile or forgiving--you had to fly the Crusader. The aircraft was very responsive, to the point that inexperience or a lack of feel for the aircraft could mean trouble. As with any airplane, it was common at first to "underfly" it. But with experience, it was truly awesome!

From the first, the Crusader was impressive to fly. It

Two of VF-84's F-8Cs are shown here in low level flight. The unit's famous yellow and red flame markings around the intake are difficult to see in the photograph. *(U.S. Navy via Davis)*

went from subsonic to supersonic flight smoothly. In burner it would stay above Mach 1 pulling G's. The first afterburner take-off and climb were awesome. From the moment you lit the burner, the acceleration did not stop. There was a quick acceleration to 450 knots, then pulling the nose up for (what seemed like the first time) a rocket ride to 40,000 feet. The first maximum speed run was also very impressive. At 40,000 feet you lit the burner, and it started to move out. In level flight it smoothly moved into the Mach 1.9 range. This was the first carrier-based fighter that would exceed 1,000 miles per hour in level flight. I had an F8U-2N over 1,200 miles per hour on one flight. That is pushing Mach 2.

The Crusader was not a simple or quick airplane to master. It took several hundred hours to really learn to fly it as it was meant to be flown. The one area above all others to master was ACM (Air Combat Maneuvering). The aircraft was not for the timid, nor was it forgiving of mistakes. In subsonic flight, high speed, high G turns would often be in buffet in order to achieve maximum turn rate. When maneuvering in this area, you were very close to high speed stall, and a high speed stall in the Crusader was appropriately called a "departure," meaning the aircraft completely departed from the path of flight it had just been in. This was a violent arcing pitch-up and roll opposite to the flight path, causing a very high loss of airspeed. Unless corrected, the aircraft would immediately progress into a spin, and, for several reasons, intentional spins were not done in the Crusader.

I experienced and witnessed several departures, but one was more spectacular than the rest. Two of us were practicing a maneuver designed to force an aggressor aircraft from off of your tail to in front of you. The aggressor aircraft is allowed to overtake and move into what is gun range. Then the target aircraft makes a high G barrel roll to force the aggressor out in front, thus changing the advantage. The rudder was used to turn under maximum G conditions because the ailerons would induce a depar-

ture. On this particular occasion, I was the aggressor and LT Don Benton was the target. As I moved into gun range, Don initiated his roll. The nose came hard up and his aircraft started a sharp right roll. The next second, his nose snapped up and he spun out to the left. It was a REAL departure! I pulled up to avoid hitting him and momentarily lost him. I picked him up again below me, now upright and stable. A few seconds passed, then a spout of flame came from his tailpipe, followed by an appropriate expletive over the radio. When we were back on the ground, Don said that when he departed, he brought his throttle back to idle, and after recovering, he started pushing the throttle forward again, but it would not move because he had put it into the "engine off" position. Realizing this, he shoved it forward inadvertently into afterburner. When it lit, there was such an explosion he thought the engine had blown up. It impressed us both. But that was what it was all about--to push it to the edge.

This excellent aerial view provides a good look at VF-84's yellow and black markings. The aircraft is F-8C, 145558. *(U.S. Navy via Davis)*

This amazing sequence of photographs shows an F-8C of VF-84 taking the barricade on board the USS INDEPEN-
DENCE. The part of the hook that catches the wire came off of the tail hook, so the only choice that would save the
aircraft was a barrier engagement. In this photograph, the aircraft is through the barrier while still airborne.

(U.S. Navy via Davis)

Since the pilot had jettisoned fuel prior to landing, the Crusader was light when it touched down, and when light during
a carrier landing, it could float a little. With his nose still in the air, the F-8C is now coming to a stop during the barrier
runout. Note the early spoked nose wheel.

(U.S. Navy via Davis)

These two photographs show the aircraft after it came to a rest. Noteworthy is the damage to the vertical stabilizer. The
pilot was unhurt.

(U.S. Navy via Davis)

Four F-8Cs from VF-84 are shown taxiing out for take-off from a shore base. The date is October 8, 1960.

(U.S. Navy via Davis)

Another area of flight that demanded more than average respect was the landing phase. The F8U had the reputation of being a harder than average airplane to land aboard a carrier. In the landing configuration it was still a fairly "clean" airplane, not a "high drag" configuration moving through the air. Making small power changes resulted in a relatively slow speed change. This could catch up with you at the wrong time. One particular demonstration of "how not to handle a Crusader" happened to a student I had when I instructed with VF-174, the east coast Crusader training squadron. It was his first flight in the airplane, and as normal, we went over everything we would do and how the aircraft would feel and respond to him during each maneuver. As instructor, I flew in formation with him to see and feel how he handled the aircraft. Beginning with the take-off, and then on into the flight, he was over-controlling the nose and being rough with the aircraft. I talked repeatedly to him over the radio to smooth out and not jerk the stick. It helped some. After doing high altitude work, the next phase called for descending to 2,000 feet and putting the aircraft into the landing configuration. We would then simulate landing approaches to get a feel for the aircraft before returning for actual landings. There were some low clouds that morning, so instead of using 1,000 feet as the simulated ground, we used 5,000 feet. We came into the "break" at 6,500 feet at 300 knots. At 220 knots, out came the gear, then the leading edge devices extended and the wing started up. The next second he was flat on his back (INVERTED) with the nose about thirty degrees down.

When the wing had moved away from the fuselage, he had jerked back on the stick, stalling the aircraft. My first thought was to tell him to eject, but the nose continued smoothly down until he was vertical. I told him to put the throttle full forward, and when the engine accelerated, I told him to pull back SMOOTHLY on the stick. I repeated "smoothly" loud and clear several times as he pulled through the maneuver. I know he had 300 knots when he came out at the bottom. It was the only smooth thing he did all day long. A similar incident had just happened a short time before at the west coast training squadron, but they had not been lucky enough to have the extra altitude. The student had to eject, and did so successfully.

I flew all five fighter versions of the F8U and the photo version as well. The F8U-2N was the most impressive, because it had the best thrust-to-weight ratio. The F8U-2 was a close second. The F8U-2NE didn't turn quite as well as the earlier models, and the nose felt heavier. I think this was because it had a bigger radar. The only version I did not enjoy flying was the F8U-2NE with bomb racks added to the underside of the wings. Here was a fighter turned into a bomber that flew like a truck. The F8U-1P flew like an early version F8U. In comparison to later fighter models, it was like comparing a Model A Ford to a new sports car.

When the airplane comes up in conversation among pilots, you can tell there is a special pride among those who flew this aircraft. The Crusader was the BEST of the BEST.

CRUSADER FIGHTERS

F8U-1/F-8A

The first production version of the Crusader was the F-8A, which was originally designated the F8U-1. This aircraft belongs to VF-154, and is shown aboard the USS HANCOCK, CVA-19. Note the extended nose gear and the original spoked nose wheel. (National Archives)

The first production version of the Crusader was the F8U-1, which was later redesignated the F-8A. It first flew on September 20, 1955, and 318 were built between 1956 and 1958. The initial order had been for 448 aircraft, but the last 130 were delivered as F8U-1Es (F-8Bs). The first thirty aircraft were fitted with the Pratt & Whitney J57-P-12 engine, but this was replaced with the more powerful -4 version and in all subsequent F-8As. The original thirty were then retrofitted with the -4 as well. This made the F-8A a Mach 1.5 aircraft. Other improvements added during the production run included the addition of a retractable in-flight refueling probe in a blister on the forward left side of the fuselage. This was begun with the fiftieth production aircraft, and retrofitted to the earlier airframes. The original Vought ejection seat was replaced with the Martin Baker F5 seat.

The F-8A was armed with four 20mm cannon, thirty-two 2.75-inch rockets in a drawer in the lower fuselage, and two Sidewinder missiles could be carried on fuselage stations. The AN/APG-30 gunsight radar and fire control system was installed for weapons delivery. The first aircraft was accepted for service in December 1956, just four years and three months after the issue of the original requirement by the Navy. It was delivered to VF-32 in March 1957, with VMF-122 being the first Marine squadron to receive the Crusader. The first carrier deployment was with VF-32 on board the USS Saratoga, (CVA-60).

After being replaced with later versions of the Crusader, the F-8As were relegated to training roles, serving as advanced single-seat trainers. The designation TF-8A was often applied to these aircraft. This should not be confused with the two-seat TF-8A described below. Two F-8As were configured as DF-8As, and were used to con-

An F-8A from VF-211 drags its speed brake and jettisons fuel from its wing tips in order to bring its weight within landing limits. This photograph which is dated March 26, 1963, was taken by an RF-8A from VF-63. (U.S. Navy)

This photograph provides an overall look at the cockpit in an F-8A. Color photographs of an F-8A's cockpit can be found on page 37. (National Archives)

Underside details of the F-8A are visible in this view of a VX-3 aircraft that is being hoisted aboard a MIDWAY class carrier.
(National Archives)

trol Regulus missiles. QF-8As were used as drones themselves.

Perhaps the best known F-8A was the seventy-seventh airframe, 143710, which was brought up to F-8E standards and used as the prototype for that version. Once it completed duties in that role, it was converted again into the only two-seat Crusader ever built. It retained the IR sensor on the nose, had no rocket pack, and only two cannons. The J57-P-20 engine provided the power. It was first flown in the two-seat configuration on February 6, 1962, and was originally designated YF8U-1T. This was later changed to YTF-8A, then TF-8A. Later, while in service with NASA, it was designated NTF-8A. The aircraft was destroyed in a crash on July 28, 1978, while helping train pilots of the Philippine Air Force.

Four F-8As from VF-103 sport yellow arrows with a black outline on their tails as they fly over the USS FORRES-TAL, CVA-59, and the Mediterranean Sea on October 10, 1958.
(U.S. Navy)

An F-8M designation was to be given to F-8As that were planned in the remanufacturing program, but none were ever built. It would have retained the J57-P-4A engine. Electronics used in the F-8A are shown in the following table.

UHF Transmitter/Receiver AN/ARC-27A
UHF Direction Finder AN/ARA-25
VHF Navigation Receiver AN/ARN-14E*
IFF Transponder AN/APX-6B
Radar AN/APG-30A
Coder AN/APA-89

*AN/ARN-21 Alternate

F-8A PERFORMANCE CHARACTERISTICS

Take-off weight .... 26,969 lbs.
Fuel .... 8,275 lbs.
Payload .... 934 lbs.
Wing loading .... 71.9 lbs./sq. ft.
Stall speed-power off .... 134.8 kts.
T.O. run, S.L. (calm)* .... 5,200 ft.
T.O. run, S.L. (25 kt. wind)* .... 3,920 ft.
Max speed/altitude* .... 590 kts./2,000 ft.
Rate of climb at S.L.* .... 5,380 fpm.
Service ceiling* .... 42,300 ft.
Combat range .... 1,280 n. mi.
Average cruising speed .... 494 kts.
Combat radius/mission time .... 345 n. mi./1.73 hr.

* Military thrust, no afterburner

These performance characteristics are based on an aircraft armed with four 20mm cannon, 500 rounds of ammunition, and thirty-two 2.75-inch rockets.

Source: U.S. Navy Standard Aircraft Characteristics

F8U-1E/F-8B/F-8L

*At left is F-8B, 145492, shown making a low level pass. F-8As and F-8Bs were used for some time as advanced trainers, and this aircraft is presently being used in this role. Note both **NAVY** and **MARINE** lettered on the aft fuselage. At right is 145419 after it was remanufactured as an F-8L. The F-8L was the only remanufactured Crusader that did not have the ventral fins, although provisions were made for them. Plates covering the attachment points for the ventral fins can be seen in the photograph.*   *(Left Picciani, right Miller via Flightleader)*

The F8U-1Es were originally part of the F8U-1 order, but with the addition of the AN/APS-67 low performance search radar, these aircraft receive the "E" suffix, and were later redesignated F-8Bs. With only 130 examples being built, the -1E was built in fewer numbers than any other American version of the Crusader. Like the F8U-1, it was powered by the J57-P-4 engine. F8U-1, 145318, served as the prototype, and the first flight was made on September 3, 1958. F-8Bs served as advanced trainers during most of their operational life.

Beginning in 1968, sixty-one F-8Bs were rebuilt as F-8Ls, which was the smallest number for any remanufactured version. They were the only remanufactured Crusaders not to have ventral fins. Provisions were made for them to be added, but small plates covered the mounting holes. Looking for these plates on the lower aft fuselage is one good way to distinguish the F-8L from other versions. During the remanufacturing program for the F-8L, instrument changes were made in the cockpit to improve night flying capabilities. Approach power compensators were added, but the original engine and fire control system was retained. F-8Ls served primarily as training aircraft, but others were converted to DF-8L drones.

F-8B PERFORMANCE CHARACTERISTICS

Take-off weight	27,468 lbs.
Fuel	8,275 lbs.
Payload	1,262 lbs.
Wing loading	73.3 lbs./sq. ft.
Stall speed-power off	136.8 kts.
T.O. run, S.L. (calm)*	5,650 ft.
T.O. run, S.L. (25 kt. wind)*	4,220 ft.
Max speed/altitude*	570 kts./15,000 ft.
Rate of climb at S.L.*	3,950 fpm.
Service ceiling*	41,100 ft.
Combat range	1,150 n. mi.
Average cruising speed	494 kts.
Combat radius/mission time	310 n. mi./1.6 hr.

* Military thrust, no afterburner

These performance characteristics are based on an aircraft armed with four 20mm cannon, 500 rounds of ammunition, thirty-two 2.75-inch rockets, and two Sidewinder missiles.

Source: U.S. Navy Standard Aircraft Characteristics

These two F-8Ls have been converted to the DF-8L drone configuration as indicated by the blade antenna just aft of the canopy. The one at left is in the markings of the Naval Missile Center, and was photographed in November 1974. At right is 145450, and it is in the markings of the Pacific Missile Test Center. The photo is dated August 1977.

(Left Flightleader, right Curry via Leader)

F8U-2/F-8C/F-8K

With the rugged coastline of the Mediterranean Sea below, four F-8Cs from VF-82 and the USS SHANGRI-LA, CVA-38, fly patrol with Sidewinder missiles mounted on "Y" rails. The F-8C was the first Crusader to feature the ventral fins and the afterburner cooling scoop.

(U.S. Navy via Jones)

It was with the F8U-2 (F-8C) that the Crusader design began to really mature. There were two noticeable additions to the airframe, these being the ventral fins on the lower fuselage and the afterburner cooling scoops on the upper tail cone. Both were to become standard for the remaining fighter versions of the Crusader as well as the remanufactured RF-8G. Powered by the J57-P-16 engine, the F-8C had a marked increase in performance over the earlier versions, and was limited to Mach 1.7 only because of instability at higher speeds. F-8A, 140448, was used as the prototype, and first flew in December 1957. The first production F-8C made its first flight on August 20, 1958, with Jim Omvig at the controls. VF-84 was the first unit to receive this version, and they took deliveries beginning on April 4, 1959. During the war in Vietnam, F-8Cs scored six confirmed kills, five over MiG-17s and one over a MiG-21.

The APS-67 radar and EX-16 fire control system, for improved tracking and armament capabilities, was fitted in the F-8C. Other electronics used in this version of the

Crusader are shown in the following table.

Integrated Electronic Central AN/ASQ-17B
  (contains functions of AN/ARC-27A,
  AN/APX-6B, and AN/ARA-25)
Coder Group AN/APA-89
Radio Set (TACAN) AN/ARN-21

These two F-8Cs belong to VC-4. Markings consist of a red tail, white disc and numbers, and black letters.

(U.S. Navy)

The Marines also flew the F-8C version of the Crusader, as evidenced by this photograph. The aircraft belong to VMF-333, which was operating off the USS FORRESTAL, CVA-59, during the crisis in Lebanon.   (U.S. Navy)

Gyro Stabilized Magnetically Slaved
  Compass MA-1
Armament Control System AN/AWG-3
  (includes AN/APS-67 radar set and
  EX-16 Aircraft Fire Control System)

Beginning in December 1968, eighty-seven F-8Cs were remanufactured as F-8Ks. The airframe, particularly the wing, was strengthened so as to extend life for another 2000 catapult launchings and arrested landings. A stronger A-7 type landing gear was installed. As with

This F-8C, 146992, is shown here after it was remanufactured to F-8K standards. It is painted in the markings of the VMF-321.   *(Flightleader)*

After missing the wires, this F-8C from VF-84 floats above the deck of the USS INDEPENDENCE, CVA-62, as the pilot commits a bolter and has to go around to try again. This action occurred on August 11, 1960.   (U.S. Navy)

the F-8L, there was no upgrade in original radar and fire control systems. The engine remained the J57-P-16 or -16B version. Two pylons, like those fitted to the F-8E, were added under the wings to carry external stores, and the cockpit was upgraded to F-8E standards. F-8Ks were used primarily by reserve squadrons.

F-8C PERFORMANCE CHARACTERISTICS

Take-off weight	27,810 lbs.
Fuel	8,657 lbs.
Payload	683 lbs.
Wing loading	74.2 lbs./sq. ft.
Stall speed-power off	137.3 kts.
T.O. run, S.L. (calm)*	5,660 ft.
T.O. run, S.L. (25 kt. wind)*	4,080 ft.
Max speed/altitude*	570 kts./15,000 ft.
Rate of climb at S.L.*	4,090 fpm.
Service ceiling*	40,000 ft.
Combat range	1,195 n. mi.
Average cruising speed	495 kts.
Combat radius/mission time	300 n. mi./1.56 hr.

* Military thrust, no afterburner

These performance characteristics are based on an aircraft armed with four 20mm cannon, 500 rounds of ammunition, and two Sidewinder missiles.

Source: U.S. Navy Standard Aircraft Characteristics

F8U-2N/F-8D/F-8H

There is always a clown in every group--or squadron! These two F-8Ds are from VF-154 and the USS CORAL SEA, CVA-43. The photograph was taken in January 1962 over the Philippines. Note the IR sensor on the noses of these two aircraft. *(U.S. Navy)*

The fastest Crusader variant was the F-8D, which had originally been designated the F8U-2N. The increased power came from the J57-P-20 engine, which was also used in the later F-8E. However, the F-8E's heavier weight degraded performance by a rather small margin over that achieved by the F-8D. The "N" suffix was added to the original designation to denote a "night" or all weather capability that was achieved with the addition of the Magnavox AN/APQ-83 radar. This radar could provide illumination for the AIM-9C radar-homing version of the Sidewinder missile. It was with the F-8D that the "Y" racks for doubling the Sidewinder missile load from two to four made its initial appearance. Two AIM-9Cs paired with two AIM-9Bs would give the F-8D an IR and radar homing capability. But the AIM-9C did not gain much success, and the Navy opted for the radar guided AIM-7 Sparrow instead. Since the Crusader could not carry the Sparrow, it really remained a clear air fighter armed with guns and IR versions of the Sidewinder. The rocket drawer was deleted, and the resulting space was used to expand the internal fuel capacity by seventy-five gallons. This meant an increase from 1,273 gallons in the earlier versions to 1,348 in the F-8D and F-8E. One F-8D stayed in the air

three hours and forty minutes on internal fuel alone. The IR sensor above the nose, a standard feature of the F-8E, was also fitted to some F-8Ds.

Another improvement made to the F-8D over previous versions was the installation of Vought's "pushbutton" autopilot which provided a three-axis attitude hold and auxiliary altitude hold and bank control features. Electronics fitted to the F-8D were as shown in the following table.

Integrated Electronic Central AN/ASQ-17B
  (contains functions of AN/ARC-27A,
  AN/APX-6B, and AN/ARA-25)
Coder Group AN/APA-89
Radio Set (TACAN) AN/ARN-21
Gyro Stabilized Magnetically
  Slaved Compass MA-1

One of the primary missions of the Crusader was to protect the fleet. Here, F-8D, 148639, intercepts a Tu-16 Badger bomber in Egyptian markings. The bomber was trying to take a peek at the NATO exercise "Dawn Patrol" on May 3, 1969. The F-8D is from VF-13 and the USS SHANGRI-LA. *(U.S. Navy)*

One of the last three F-8Ds built, 148708, is shown here in the markings of VF-62 and the USS SHANGRI-LA. This photograph was taken in March 1968. *(Garrett)*

Armament Control System AN/AWG-4
  (includes AN/APQ-83 radar set
  and EX-16 aircraft fire control
  system)

The first flight of an F-8D took place on February 16, 1960, with John Konrad at the controls. A total of 152 were built between 1960 and 1962. VF-111 was the first squadron to receive the F-8D, beginning on June 1, 1960. F-8Ds were used by only one squadron in Vietnam, and that was VF-154 as part of Air Wing 15 on board the USS Coral Sea, CVA-43. This cruise was in the early war years of 1964-65, and no MiG kills were scored. It was the only cruise of the war in which a Crusader fighter squadron was not embarked aboard an Essex class carrier.

In 1967 and 1968, eighty-nine F-8Ds were remanufactured as F-8Hs, the first of which was flown by John Konrad on July 17, 1967. In addition to a strengthened airframe, the landing gear was replaced with the stronger A-7 type, the tail hook was strengthened, and the Bullpup avionics hump was added on top of the wing and fuselage center section. Pylons were added to a strengthened wing so that more external stores could be carried to attack ground targets. A CP-742A/APQ deviated pursuit computer and AN/ASA-63 Missile Acquisition Programmer allowed the launching of AIM-9D missiles with lead on the target. SHOEHORN equipment provisions were made for electronic warning and countermeasures. The J57-P-420 engine replaced the -20 used in the F-8D.

Three Vietnam War cruises were made with the F-8H, two by VF-51, and one by VF-24. VF-51 scored two victories over MiG-21s with the F-8H, and these were the only kills made by this version of the Crusader.

Eighty-nine F-8Ds were remanufactured to F-8H standards. This is F-8H, 148659, in the markings of VF-202, which is one of the Naval Reserve Squadrons. The photograph was taken on February 14, 1976.

(Knowles via Leader)

F-8D PERFORMANCE CHARACTERISTICS

Take-off weight .... 29,472 lbs.
Fuel .... 9,167 lbs.
Payload .... 983 lbs.
Wing loading .... 78.6 lbs./sq. ft.
Stall speed-power off .... 144 kts.
T.O. run, S.L. (calm)* .... 6,980 ft.
T.O. run, S.L. (25 kt. wind)* .... 5,160 ft.
Max speed/altitude* .... 589 kts./5,000 ft.
Rate of climb at S.L.* .... 5,860 fpm.
Service ceiling* .... 40,550 ft.
Combat range .... 1,263 n. mi.
Average cruising speed .... 495 kts.
Combat radius .... 355 n. mi.

* Military thrust, no afterburner

These performance characteristics are based on an aircraft armed with four 20mm cannon, 500 rounds of ammunition, and four Sidewinder missiles.

The instrument panel of an F-8D is shown in this photograph. The variable stability system control panel (also called the automatic flight control system panel) is visible in the center of the photo. *(U.S. Navy)*

This is the instrument panel after remanufacture to F-8H standards. There is considerable difference between this and the former F-8D panel seen at left.

F8U-2NE/F-8E/F-8J

*This F-8E, 149167, is the CAG aircraft for VF-174 and CVW-4. **Commander Carrier Air Wing Four** is written under the wing in Old English, and multi-colored stripes are on the rudder. **Capt. Jim Ferris** is lettered on the side of the cockpit. This early F-8E does not have the Bullpup guidance fairing on the top of the fuselage.* (Baldwin)

The final fighter variant of the Crusader as originally built was the F-8E. It differed from the F-8D in three major areas. First, it had the larger AN/APQ-94 radar which required a larger radome. This radome also had the added advantage of improving the intake pressure recovery, and increased the length of the airframe three inches. Second, underwing pylons were added to carry a variety

One F-8E from VF-103 is shown on the number one cat aboard the USS FORRESTAL, while two others wait for their turn to launch. An F-4B is waiting behind the blast shield for cat two, while another Phantom can be seen on the elevator at the extreme right of the photograph. An A-4E Skyhawk from VMA-331 has just been launched from one of the waist catapults, and can be seen just above the steam left by the launch of a departing Phantom. This photograph was taken on January 11, 1965. (U.S. Navy)

of weapons for attacking ground targets. Third, and directly related to one of those underwing weapons, was a fairing on top of the wing and fuselage center section that housed a transmitter to control the Bullpup guided missile. Also, the AAS-15 IR sensor became a standard feature on the nose above the radome. Electronics fitted in the F-8E were as follows.

Integrated Electronic Central .... A/NAS Q/17B
   (contains functions of AN/ARC-27A,
   AN/APX-6B, and AN/ARA-25)
Coder Group AN/APA-98
Radio Set (TACAN) AN/APA-52
Radar Altimeter AN/APN-22
Gyro Stabilized Magnetically
   Slaved Compass MA-1
Armament Control System AN/AWG-4
   (includes AN/APQ-94 Radar Set
   and EX-16 Aircraft Fire
   Control System)
Autopilot CV/AES-6
IR System AN/AAS-15
Bullpup Transmitter AN/ARW-77
Fuse Control AN/AWW-1

Eleven MiGs fell to F-8Es over Vietnam. All were MiG-17s except for one MiG-21.

F-8A, 143710, served as the F-8E prototype, and first flew on June 30, 1961. It was later converted to the two-seat YTF-8A. The first production F-8E made its maiden flight in September of that same year. A total of 286 F-8Es were built before Crusader production finally ended.

This excellent photograph shows details of the F-8E. Note the addition of detachable wing pylons. When built as F-8Es, the aircraft had the single hinged leading edge droop. (LTV via Jones)

The most capable of all Crusaders was the F-8J, which was the remanufactured version of the F-8E. A total of 136 airframes were updated to this standard beginning in January 1968, and the F-8J received the most in the way of improvements during remanufacture. The first flight of an F-8J was made on January 31, 1968. The J57-P-420 engine was fitted after 1970, the wing was strengthened for increased service life of 4000 more hours, and the landing gear and arresting hook were improved to A-7 standards. Provisions were made to carry external fuel. The larger horizontal tail, used on the French Crusaders, replaced the smaller one used on all other American variants. Another French feature, the double hinged leading edge droop, was added in conjunction with a blowing type of boundary layer control (BLC) system in the upper leading edge surface of the ailerons and inboard flaps. This increased high lift capability in the low speed flight regime and reduced take-off and landing speeds by fifteen knots. An AN/APQ-124 radar improved detection and attack capability, and the AN/ASA-63 Missile Acquisition Programmer allowed the launching of AIM-9D missiles with lead on the target.

F-8E PERFORMANCE CHARACTERISTICS

Take-off weight .... 29,756 lbs.
Fuel .... 9,167 lbs.
Payload .... 983 lbs.
Wing loading .... 79.3 lbs./sq. ft.
Stall speed-power off .... 144.9 kts.
T.O. run, S.L. (calm)* .... 7,200 ft.
T.O. run, S.L. (25 kt. wind)* .... 5,300 ft.
Max speed/altitude* .... 584 kts./1,000 ft.
Rate of climb at S.L.* .... 5,590 fpm.
Service ceiling* .... 40,000 ft.
Combat range .... 1,238 n. mi.
Average cruising speed .... 495 kts.
Combat radius/mission time** ..... 150 n. mi./1.71 hr.

* Military thrust, no afterburner
** Combat air patrol mission near ship/base

These performance characteristics are based on an aircraft armed with four 20mm cannon, 500 rounds of ammunition, and four Sidewinder missiles.

Source: U.S. Navy Standard Aircraft Characteristics

An F-8E from VF-11 eases up to the number 1 catapult aboard the USS FRANKLIN D. ROOSEVELT, CVA-42, during flight operations off the coast of Guantanamo, Cuba, on January 19, 1964. An A-4 Skyhawk from VA-12 is almost ready to go on cat two. (U.S. Navy)

One hundred and thirty-six F-8Es were remanufactured to F-8Js. The most noticeable change was the addition of the double-hinged leading edge droops that had been used on the French Crusaders. The double-hinged droop is clearly visible in this photograph of an F-8J from VF-194 and the USS ORISKANY, CVA-34. (Flightleader)

CRUSADER DETAILS

CANOPY

The windscreen and canopy are seen from above in this view. The tops of the cockpit walls where the canopy closed onto the fuselage were usually painted black.

(U.S. Navy)

This front view provides a look at the details of the windscreen. Three rear view mirrors that are located at the forward end of the canopy are contrasted against the light wall in the background.

Center left: The right side canopy hinge and some details of the canopy rails are visible here. The inside of the canopy framing was painted flat black. (Flightleader)

Center right: The canopy releasing latch is shown here in this left side view.

Left: The area behind the seat is shown in this photograph taken from the right side. The cylinder that raises and lowers the canopy is visible in the center. Also note the rubber strip that seals the canopy to the fuselage for cockpit pressurization.

EJECTION SEAT

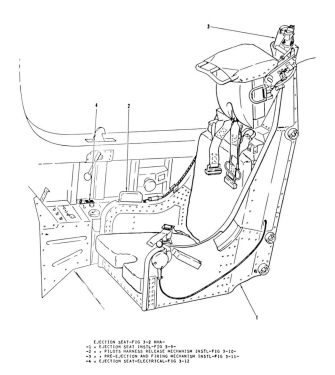

EJECTION SEAT-FIG 3-2 NHA-
-1 • EJECTION SEAT INSTL-FIG 3-9-
-2 • PILOTS HARNESS RELEASE MECHANISM INSTL-FIG 3-10-
-3 • PRE-EJECTION AND FIRING MECHANISM INSTL-FIG 3-11-
-4 • EJECTION SEAT-ELECTRICAL-FIG 3-12

This is the Vought ejection seat used in the prototypes and early production versions of the Crusader. The seat was dark gull gray, except for the headrest, which was black.

MK-F7 EJECTION SEAT COMPONENTS

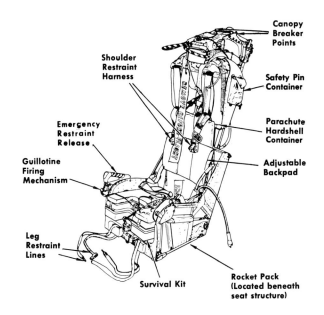

Canopy Breaker Points

Shoulder Restraint Harness

Safety Pin Container

Emergency Restraint Release

Parachute Hardshell Container

Guillotine Firing Mechanism

Adjustable Backpad

Leg Restraint Lines

Survival Kit

Rocket Pack (Located beneath seat structure)

When the change to MK-F5 was made, Vought was a year away from fielding a rocket kit for their seat. F-8 pilots then had to wait until April 1968 for the Martin Baker MK-F7 rocket seat to be fitted in the Crusader.

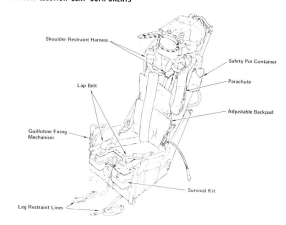

Shoulder Restraint Harness

Safety Pin Container

Parachute

Adjustable Backpad

Lap Belt

Guillotine Firing Mechanism

Survival Kit

Leg Restraint Lines

The Martin Baker MK-F5 replaced the Vought seat, beginning with the first F8U-2NE. In the first half of 1962, refit kits were supplied for the earlier versions. This required making the cockpit wider by several inches between the consoles, and this was a considerable problem. It was like trying to fit a square peg in a round hole.

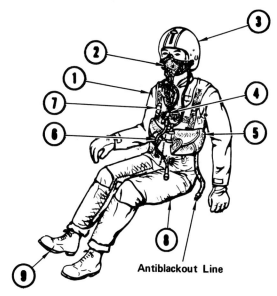

Antiblackout Line

1. **Coveralls, flying, summer, fire resistant, type CS/FRP**
   or
   Coveralls, flying, anti-exposure, Mk-5A, (not shown)
2. **Mask, oxygen, type A-13A with retainer and release assy**
3. **Helmet, pilot's protective, type APH-6**
4. **Regulator aviator's miniature oxygen, breathing**
5. **Life preserver, inflatable, Mk-3C**
6. **Oxygen hose assembly mini-regulator to seat pan P/N 33C1138**
   or
   Oxygen hose assembly — RSSK to mini-reg, P/N 33C1178, and mini-reg to seat pan
7. **Harness, integrated parachute, MS-22015**
8. **Suit, Antiblackout, Mk-2A**
9. **Boots, flying, impact resistant**

NOSE LANDING GEAR

The nose gear on an early F8U-1 is shown here. It is basically the same as used on production aircraft and shows the early spoked wheel. The forward nose gear door was changed, having three approach attitude indicator lights added.
(National Archives)

The forward nose gear door with the approach indicator lights is illustrated here. This is the landing gear as used on Crusaders prior to remanufacture. *(May)*

Compare this photo of the nose gear on an RF-8G to the photograph of the nose gear on a fighter version at right. Because of the camera fairing immediately ahead of the nose gear, there was no forward nose gear door on the RF-8. Instead, the forward portion of the two side doors had a curvature added that mated with the aft end of the camera fairing when the doors were closed. Also note the later and more common solid wheel design.

After remanufacture, Crusaders were fitted with the stronger A-7 type landing gear. However, the bridle launch system was still used rather than the nose tow system, so no catapult launch bar was added.

This view provides an overall look at the nose gear used on remanufactured fighter versions of the Crusader.

Details of the inside of the forward nose gear door are shown here, as seen from the right. Note the strut that actuates the door. *(May)*

This view looks forward into the nose wheel well in the Naval Aviation Museum's F-8A. It reveals the original production nose gear assembly as used on the Crusader.

This view is similar to the one in the top right photo, but was taken in the nose gear well of a remanufactured RF-8G. It illustrates the stronger gear used on remanufactured aircraft.

This photograph looks up and aft from the front left corner of the same well as seen in the photo at left. All three wheel wells were usually painted gloss white.

LEFT MAIN LANDING GEAR

A general view of the left main landing gear is provided here. Standard markings, more often seen on the gray over white scheme, are clearly visible.

This head-on view shows the angle of the gear doors when open.

This low view provides a look up and aft into the wheel well. One difference between the fighter and recon versions was that the approach indicator lights for the recon versions were located on a box on the top strut of the left main gear as seen here. This was because the RF-8s did not have a forward nose gear door on which to mount these lights. The fighter gear would look exactly the same as shown here except that the box with the lights would not be present.

The aft strut and its small door are visible in this rear photo.

Single point refueling was accomplished through a receptacle in the left main gear well.

Details of the forward end of the wheel well are revealed here.

RIGHT MAIN LANDING GEAR

The A-7 type wheel and gear used on remanufactured Crusaders is shown in this close-up of the right main landing gear.

The inside of the same wheel is shown here, and part of the brake system is clearly visible.

This front view shows the landing light located on the upper door of the right main landing gear.

This is a rear view of the right main landing gear. Hydraulic lines are visible on the main and aft struts.

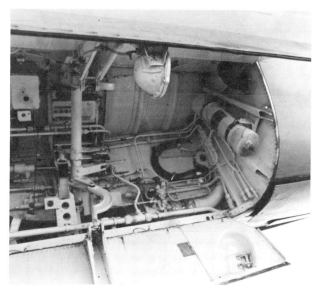

Details of the right main landing gear well are visible in these two photographs. The view at left looks aft, while the photo at right shows the forward end of the well.

ENGINE DETAILS

Various versions of Pratt & Whitney's J57 engine powered the different versions of the Crusader. Access for maintenance was gained by removing the entire tail section as one unit. Also visible in this view is the original style of the main landing gear wheel used on the F-8. (National Archives)

The right side view of the aft portion of the engine is shown here. It is installed in an RF-8G.

This is a Pratt & Whitney J57 engine displayed in the Naval Aviation Museum. The front of the engine is to the left in the photograph, and the tail pipe and afterburner have been removed.

The convergent/divergent nozzle is illustrated here. The fuselage skin around the afterburner was usually left unpainted bare metal. (May)

This view looks right up the tail pipe of a fully installed engine.

CRUSADER COLORS

A special ceremony marked the retirement of the last U.S. Navy Crusader in March 1987. The first Crusader prototype, now on display at the National Air and Space Museum, was moved to nearby NAS Andrews for the occasion. It is shown on the right in the bare metal scheme which was used on the prototypes. The RF-8G at left is painted in the last scheme used on any U.S. Navy Crusader, and that is the two-tone blue/gray tactical scheme.   *(Ostrowski via Leader)*

The colors and markings of the first prototype XF8U-1, 138899, are illustrated in these two photographs. This is the same aircraft shown on the right in the photograph above.   *(Both National Archives via Piet)*

These two photographs show the third production F8U-1, 140446, which was used for carrier qualifications aboard the USS Forrestal (CVA-59). Although this is a production aircraft, the cannon ports are still covered as they were on the prototypes.   *(Both National Archives via Piet)*

Another early production F8U-1 is seen here. Note the lack of the refueling probe blister and the faired-over gun ports. Like the prototypes and other early production F8U-1s that were used for testing, this aircraft remains in an overall bare metal scheme with colorful trim.

(National Archives via Piet)

The flaming intake and eyeball mean that this F-8C belonged to VF-84 during its first cruise with the Crusader aboard the USS INDEPENDENCE. (U.S. Navy)

The only two-seat Crusader was painted in the gull gray over white scheme with orange on the nose, wings, and tail when this photograph was taken at the Naval Air Test Center on February 21, 1975. The aircraft was destroyed in a crash three and one-half years later. (Flightleader)

This F-8A, 143682, was converted to a QF-8 and assigned to VC-8. It is painted in standard blue, yellow, and red target tug colors. (Stewart via Leader)

Another scheme used on the Crusader was the overall gull gray scheme with subdued or low visibility markings. This F-8J, 150661, was assigned to recon squadron VFP-63, and was photographed at El Paso IAP on July 20, 1980.

(Hebrok)

NASA CRUSADERS

NASA flew Crusaders to develop and study new technology and aviation hardware. These two photographs show N802NA, which was used to test a digital fly-by-wire system. *(Both Flightleader)*

N810NA is the subject of these two photographs. It was fitted with a supercritical wing and painted in standard NASA colors of white, medium blue, and dark blue. *(Left Flightleader, right Roth via Leader)*

TF-8A, formerly F-8A, 145385, became N816NA, and was leased to NASA for testing. *(Lock via Leader)*

F-8J, 149163, is shown here in the markings of VF-24 and the USS HANCOCK. It illustrates the gull gray over white scheme and colorful markings used on the Crusader throughout most of its service life.   (Flightleader)

Training versions of the AIM-9L Sidewinder are mounted on the right "Y" rack. The Crusader usually carried earlier versions of the missile.   (U.S. Navy)

The access panel for the left side guns is open, revealing feed chute, gun colors, and details.

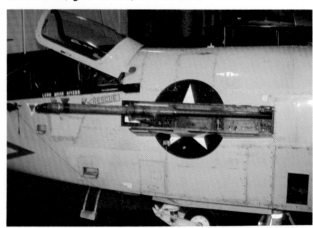

The colors and differences between the refueling probes on the fighter versions of the Crusader (left) and the recon version (right) are illustrated in these two views. The probe on the fighter versions was located in a blister on the side of the fuselage, and the covering door was hinged at the top. On the recon version, the probe was mounted inside the fuselage rather than in a blister, and the door was hinged at the bottom.   (Left Flightleader, right Kinzey)

FIGHTER COCKPITS

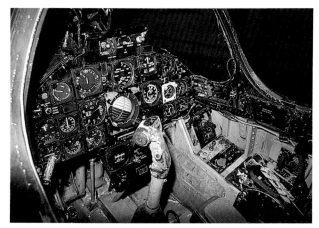

The six photographs on this page illustrate the differences in the cockpits of the earliest F-8A and the F-8J versions. The three photographs on the left side of the page were taken in an F-8A, while the three corresponding photographs on the right side of the page are of an F-8J cockpit. At left is the F-8A instrument panel, and at right is the instrument panel in an F-8J.

The left console of the F-8A is at left, and compares to the F-8J on the right.

This is the right console in the F-8A.

The F-8J's right console is similar, but differences do exist.

RF-8 COLORS

As was the case on the fighter versions of the Crusader, paint schemes used on the recon versions ranged from the very colorful to the overly subdued. The Bi-centennial markings used on VFP-63's RF-8Gs are shown here. The aircraft remains in the gull gray over white scheme.
(Lock via Leader)

Another VFP-63 aircraft is shown a split second before launch. Note the "Eyes of the Fleet" art on the forward end of the wing. (U.S. Navy)

Early markings for VFP-62 are shown on this RF-8A.
(U.S. Navy)

The overall gull gray scheme is illustrated on this RF-8G assigned to Reserve Squadron VFP-306.

The tactical gray scheme was used for a short time on the last RF-8Gs left in service. The darker top color is FS 36320, and the lighter lower color is FS 36375. This aircraft belongs to VFP-206, which was the last U.S. Navy squadron to operate any version of the Crusader.

RF-8G COCKPIT

Above: This is the instrument panel in an RF-8G.

Left: The left console is quite similar to that seen in the fighter versions on page 37.

The right console also shares a lot in common with its fighter counterparts.

Details of the control column are revealed here.

FOREIGN CRUSADERS

The first scheme used on French Crusaders was the same gull gray over white scheme used on the U.S. Navy's F-8s. This aircraft has a Matra Missile on the fuselage station. *(Flightleader)*

The French then went to the overall gray scheme as shown here. The aircraft in the photograph at right has a Matra Magic missile on the left fuselage station. *(Both Flightleader)*

Aircraft delivered to the Philippine Air Force were originally delivered in a two-tone gray scheme that appears to be dark gull gray over light gull gray. Both colors were glossy, and are visible in the photograph at left. They have since been repainted in a rather crude wraparound camouflage as seen at right. *(Left Huston, right Anido)*

DIMENSIONS AND DRAWINGS

DIMENSION	ACTUAL MEASUREMENT	1/100th SCALE	1/72nd SCALE*	1/48th SCALE	1/32nd SCALE
Length F-8A, -B, -C, -D	54' 2.75"	6.51"	9.04"	13.55"	20.33"
Length F-8E	54' 5.75"	6.54"	9.08"	13.61"	20.43"
Length RF-8A	54' 6.10"	6.54"	9.08"	13.62"	20.44"
Wingspan (extended)	35' 8"	4.28"	5.94"	8.92"	13.38"
Wingspan (folded)	22' 6"	2.70"	3.75"	5.63"	8.44"
Height (to top of tail)	12' 1"	1.45"	2.01"	3.02"	4.53"
Wheel Base (fighters)	18' 1"	2.17"	3.01"	4.52"	6.78"
Wheel Base (RF-8)	18' 1.82"	2.18"	3.03"	4.54"	6.81"
Wheel Tread	9' 8"	1.16"	1.61"	2.42"	3.63"
Horizontal Tail Span	18' 2"	2.18"	3.03"	4.54"	6.81"
Horizontal Tail Span (F-8J and French)	19' 3.9"	2.32"	3.22"	4.83"	7.25"

* For 1/144th scale, divide 1/72nd scale measurements in half.

These measurements apply to all the aircraft except as noted, and to the corresponding remanufactured aircraft for the models given. The one exception is the horizontal tail span of the F-8J (a remanufactured F-8E). This measurement for the F-8J is given in the table.

Scale measurements are given to the nearest 1/100th of an inch.

Source: Standard Aircraft Characteristics, U.S. Navy.

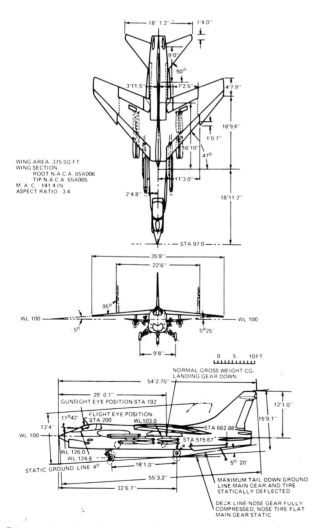

Dimensions for the earlier F-8 versions are shown in this three-view drawing.   (U.S. Navy)

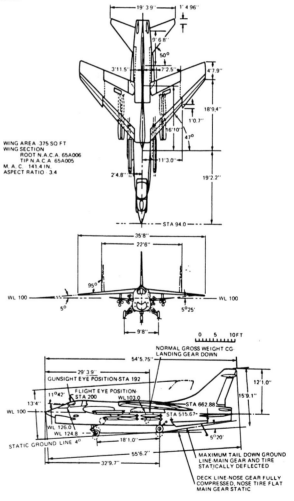

Dimensions for the F-8E and F-8J are shown here. The increased length is due to the larger radome. Measurements given for the horizontal tail are for the enlarged tail plane used on the F-8J. The F-8E has the smaller horizontal tail, as reflected in the drawings to the left.

(U.S. Navy)

41

F-8E FIVE VIEW 1/72nd SCALE DRAWING

Dana Bell

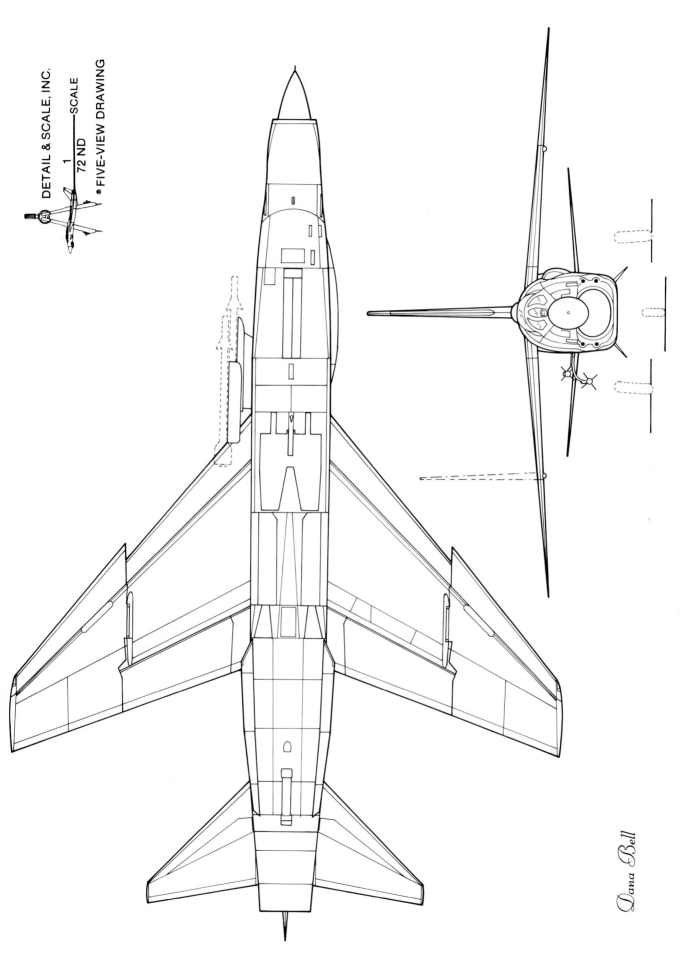

DETAIL & SCALE, INC.

1
———
72 ND SCALE

® FIVE-VIEW DRAWING

Dana Bell

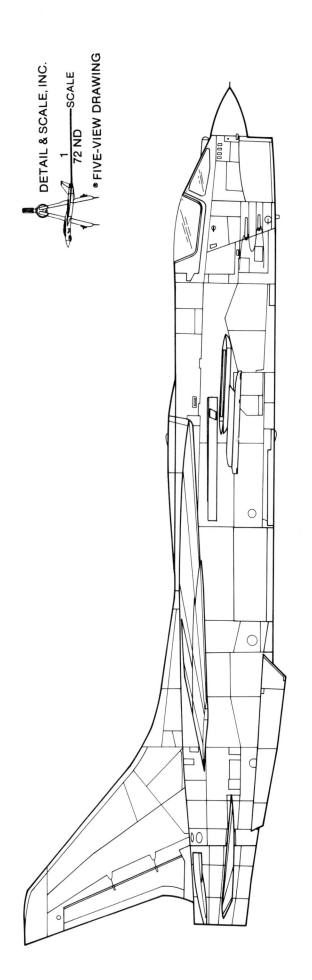

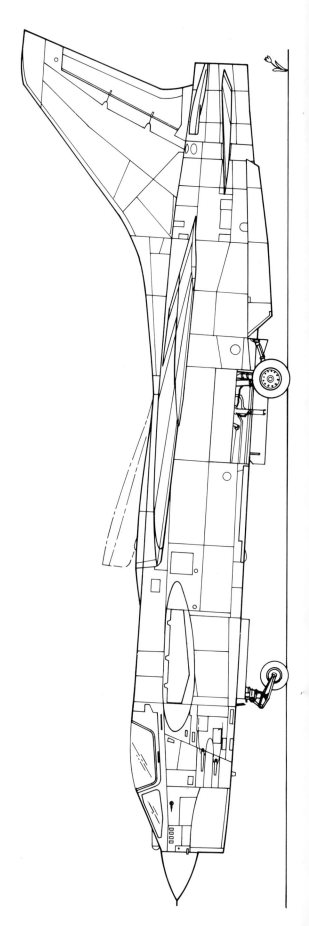

Dana Bell

RF-8A LEFT SIDE VIEW

Dana Bell

DETAIL & SCALE, INC.

1 —— SCALE
72 ND

® FIVE-VIEW DRAWING

RF-8A LOWER FORWARD FUSELAGE

TF-8A LEFT SIDE VIEW

BLACK
DAY-GLO

BLACK LETTERS

NAVY

DROGUE
CHUTE
COMPARTMENT

BLACK LETTERS

BLACK OUTLINE
WHITE BACKGROUND

LIGHT

TF-8A CANOPY TOP VIEW

DAY-GLO

RED

BLACK

Drawing Courtesy of Vought Aeronautics

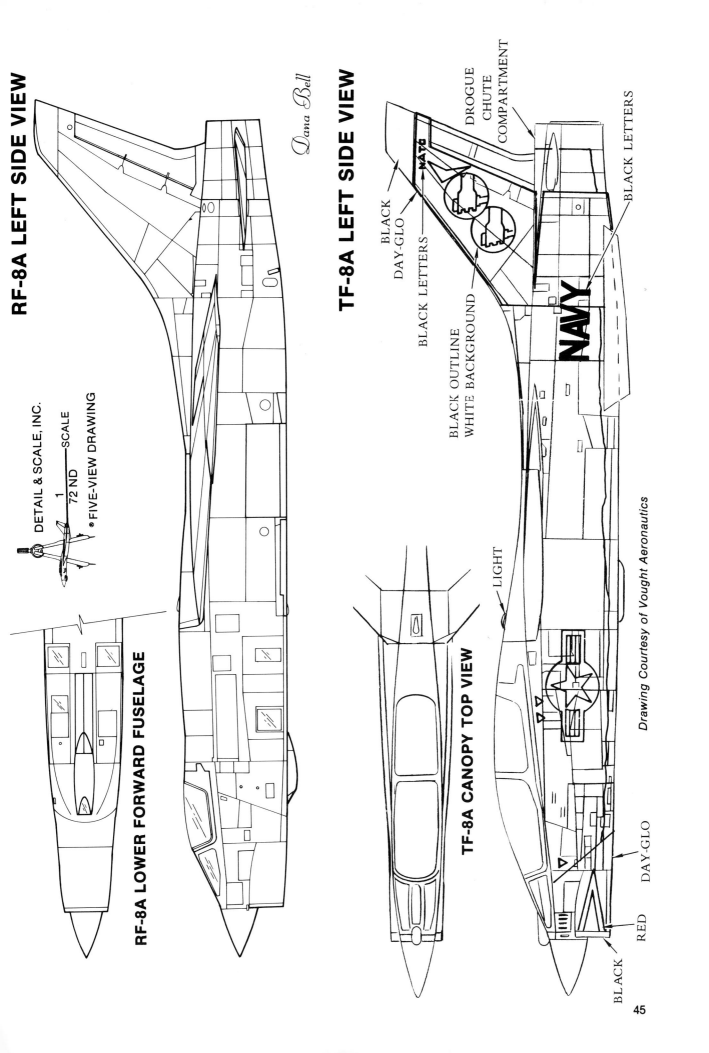

FUSELAGE DETAILS

This right side view of the nose is shown here with markings used on the gull gray over white scheme visible. This is an F-8H. (Flightleader)

The retractable boarding step and the two fold down steps/hand holds are visible in this photograph. Two probes, one just behind the radome, and one at the top of the 3, can also be seen. This aircraft is also an F-8H.

The sharp, thin leading edge of the intake and the bulges for the guns are shown from this angle. (Flightleader)

The electrical connection for ground power is located just aft of the retractable step on the left side of the forward fuselage section.

The oxygen system is replenished on the right side of the forward fuselage just above the guns. (U.S. Navy)

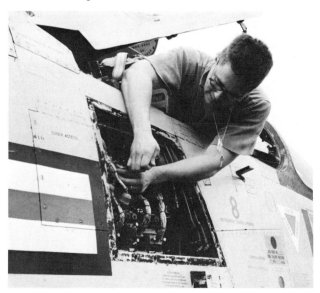

An aviation electrician's mate is performing electrical maintenance on an F-8J from VF-51 on board the USS BON HOMME RICHARD. (U.S. Navy)

Under the radome was---another radome! These two aviation fire control technicians are working on the radar of an F-8J from VF-53.   (U.S. Navy)

This view looks down the intake back to the engine. The interior of the intake was usually painted gloss white.

A distinctive feature of the Crusader was the exhaust for the heat exchanger and refrigeration turbine that was located on the right side of the fuselage. On quite a few aircraft, the raised rectangular area was painted flat black.

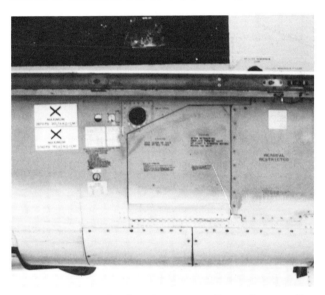

The servicing point for the pneumatic system on the fighter versions was located on the right side of the fuselage below the heat exchanger exhaust and the launch rail.

Before the addition of the ventral strakes, a saber drain was located on the aft left fuselage.

The shape of the left ventral strake is shown to good effect in this view. These strakes first made their appearance on the F-8C, and were on all remanufactured Crusaders except the F-8L. Although provisions were made to add the strakes to the F-8L, they were never fitted.

SPEED BRAKE DETAIL

A speed brake was mounted on the lower fuselage just forward of the main landing gear. On the earlier versions of the Crusader, it was attached to the rocket drawer, as shown in these two views. The outline of the drawer is clearly visible in the photograph at left. The inside details of the brake can be seen to good effect in the right photo. The inside of the brake was usually painted gloss red.

(Both May)

After the rocket drawer was deleted, the speed brake was hinged directly to the fuselage as shown here. Note the change to the interior of the fuselage above the brake as compared to the drawer shown in the two photographs above.

(Both May)

On fighter versions of the Crusader, the leading edge of the speed brake was rounded as seen at left. But it was a bit more squared off on the recon versions so as to conform to the more rectangular cross section of the lower forward fuselage caused by the camera bay installation. This can be seen in the photograph at right. (Left May, right Kinzey)

WING DETAILS

Wing details are visible in these two views of F8U-1, 140446, aboard the USS FORRESTAL. It was said, even in the flight manual, that the Crusader had a variable incidence wing, but a more accurate description would be a two-position wing. It was either up or down, and could not be set to any position between these two limits. There were no control surfaces on the trailing edge of the wing outboard of the fold line.   *(Both National Archives)*

FLAPS, AILERONS, AND DROOPS

WING INCIDENCE CHANGE

F-8H

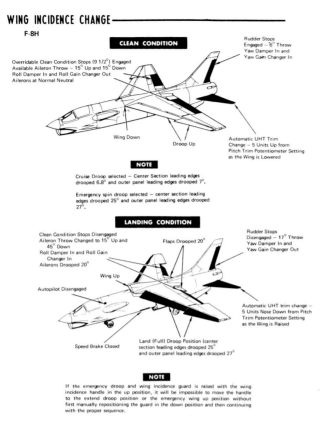

CLEAN CONDITION

Overridable Clean Condition Stops (9 1/2°) Engaged
Available Aileron Throw — 15° Up and 15° Down
Roll Damper In and Roll Gain Changer Out
Ailerons at Normal Neutral

Rudder Stops
Engaged — 6° Throw
Yaw Damper In and
Yaw Gain Changer In

Wing Down

Droop Up

Automatic UHT Trim
Change — 5 Units Up from
Pitch Trim Potentiometer
Setting as the Wing is Lowered

NOTE

Cruise Droop selected — Center Section leading edges drooped 6.8° and outer panel leading edges drooped 7°.

Emergency spin droop selected — center section leading edges drooped 25° and outer panel leading edges drooped 27°.

LANDING CONDITION

Clean Condition Stops Disengaged
Aileron Changed to 15° Up and 45° Down
Roll Damper In and Roll Gain Changer In
Ailerons Drooped 20°

Flaps Drooped 20°

Rudder Stops
Disengaged — 17° Throw
Yaw Damper In and
Yaw Gain Changer Out

Wing Up

Autopilot Disengaged

Automatic UHT trim change —
5 Units Nose Down from Pitch
Trim Potentiometer Setting
as the Wing is Raised

Speed Brake Closed

Land (Full) Droop Position (center section leading edges drooped 25° and outer panel leading edges drooped 27°

NOTE

If the emergency droop and wing incidence guard is raised with the wing incidence handle in the up position, it will be impossible to move the handle to the extend droop position or the emergency wing up position without first manually repositioning the guard in the down position and then continuing with the proper sequence.

Positions for the flying surfaces in both the clean and landing conditions are illustrated in these two drawings. This applies to all Crusader versions except the F-8J and the French F-8E (FN). *(U.S. Navy)*

F-8J

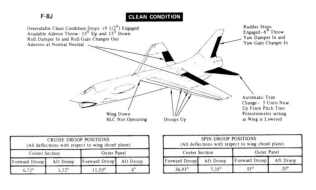

CLEAN CONDITION

Overridable Clean Condition Stops: (9 1/2°) Engaged
Available Aileron Throw: 15° Up and 15° Down
Roll Damper In and Roll Gain Changer Out
Ailerons at Normal Neutral

Rudder Stops
Engaged — 6° Throw
Yaw Damper In and
Yaw Gain Changer In

Automatic Trim
Change— 5 Units Nose
Up From Pitch Trim
Potentiometer setting
as Wing is Lowered

Wing Down
BLC Not Operating

Droops Up

CRUISE DROOP POSITIONS (All deflections with respect to wing chord plane)			
Center Section		Outer Panel	
Forward Droop	Aft Droop	Forward Droop	Aft Droop
6.72°	1.32°	11.50°	4°

SPIN DROOP POSITIONS (All deflections with respect to wing chord plane)			
Center Section		Outer Panel	
Forward Droop	Aft Droop	Forward Droop	Aft Droop
36.93°	7.35°	55°	20°

CATAPULT/BLC LANDING CONDITION

Clean Condition Stops: Disengaged
Aileron Throw: Before AFC 544, 13° Up and 49° Down; After AFC 544, 15° Up and 49° Down
Roll Damper In and Roll Gain Changer In
BLC Operating: Ailerons Drooped 40° After AFC 544, Ailerons drooped 35°

Flaps: Extended 40°; After AFC 544, Extended 30°

Rudder Stops
Disengaged—17° Throw
Yaw Damper In and
Yaw Gain Changer Out

Wing Up 5°
BLC Operating

Automatic Trim Change—
5 Units Nose Down From
Pitch Trim Potentiometer
Setting as Wing is Raised

Autopilot Disengaged   Speed Brake Closed   Land (Full) Droops

LAND (FULL) DROOP POSITIONS (All deflections with respect to wing chord plane)			
Center Section		Outer Panel	
Forward Droop	Aft Droop	Forward Droop	Aft Droop
36.93°	7.35°	55°	20°

Positions for the same surfaces are shown again in this drawing for the F-8J and F-8E (FN) with the double hinged leading edge droop and boundary layer control. *(U.S. Navy)*

Crusaders had a very narrow flap located right next to the fuselage. These two photographs show the left flap from different angles. *(Left May, right Kinzey)*

The ailerons were located outboard of the flaps and inboard of the wing fold. They could work as conventional ailerons, or could be drooped together to act as flaps when the wing was raised for take-off and landing. *(Both May)*

It seems hard to believe that the entire wing was actuated by one rather small strut at the forward right corner of the wing center section. Consider the stress on this strut when the wing was providing lift during take-offs and landings.

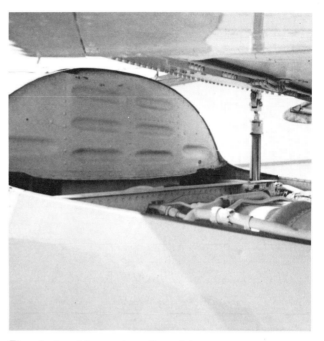

The strut and forward section of the area under the wing center section are revealed here.   (May)

Center left: This view looks aft under the raised wing, and shows details of the fuselage under the wing. The entire area and components in it are white. The photograph was taken from the forward left corner of the wing-to-fuselage joint.   (May)

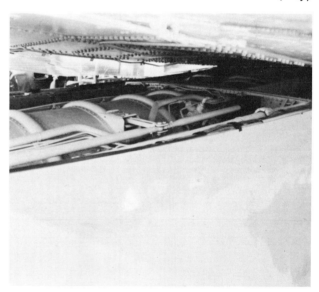

Center right: More details are visible in this photograph taken from the left side of the aircraft.   (May)

Right: The bottom skin of the center section of the wing is seen here. Tubing and fasteners are visible.   (May)

Details of the wing fold hinges are shown on this page. At left is the right fold hinge, and at right is the left wing fold.
(Left May, right Kinzey)

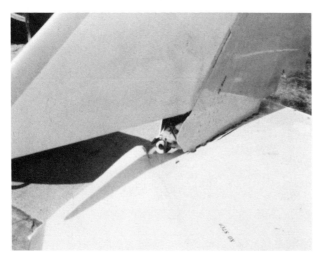

More details of the right and left wing fold hinges are revealed in these two views taken from the inside and to the front of the hinges.
(Both May)

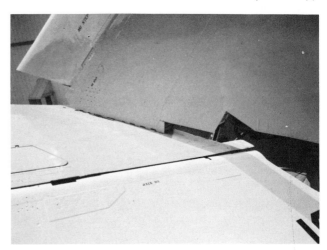

These two photographs were taken of the two hinges from the inside and behind.
(Both May)

Details of the wing tips and the navigation and formation lights are revealed here.

TAIL DETAILS

As originally built, the vertical tail of the Crusader had no ECM antennas on the leading or trailing edge. (Garrett)

During the war in Vietnam, three different ECM antenna arrangements were added to the fighter and recon versions of the Crusader. One design is shown here, and consists of a simple oval fairing attached to the trailing edge just above the rudder. (Garrett)

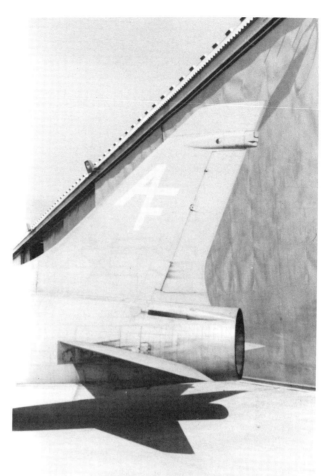

A more common and larger antenna is seen here. It faired further forward into the tail fin, and the tail light was located on the fairing.

This RF-8G has the third antenna arrangement. On the trailing edge is the same oval antenna seen in the center left photo. A large fairing is located on the leading edge of the vertical tail just ahead of it. (LTV)

This is a close-up of the afterburner cooling scoop that was added beginning with the F-8C and used on all subsequent versions. It was required because of the increase in temperature resulting from the more powerful later versions of the J57 engine.

The entire tail section of the aircraft could be removed and wheeled away from the aircraft. Open access panels provide access to the system that operates the horizontal tail.

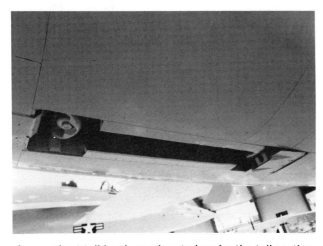

A very short tail hook was located under the tail section. This view is looking from the right side of the aircraft to the left.

There was usually a bare metal area on the fuselage where the movement of the forward half of each horizontal tail could have scraped any paint that was there. The aircraft type and BuNo were painted below this area.

The horizontal tail usually had a non-skid walkway next to the fuselage. RF-8Gs that were painted in the tactical scheme near the end of their service life were one of the rare cases where the skin around the afterburner was painted rather than being left bare metal.

More details of the retracted hook and its well can be seen here.

20MM CANNON

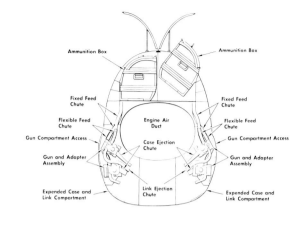

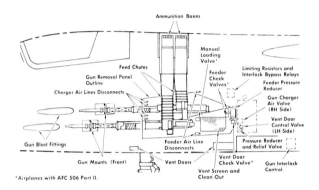

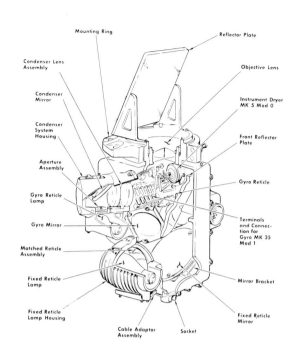

Components of the 20MM gun system arrangement are shown in this two-view diagram. (U.S. Navy)

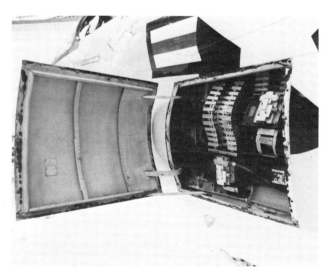

This is the left side gun bay on an F-8A. The details of the inside of the door, its hinges, and brace are all visible. Note that the lower gun is mounted further forward than the upper gun so that the ammunition chutes can clear one another.

Armament specialists are working on the right side guns of an F-8A from VF-51. Note the shape of the door and gun bay on this side as compared to the one shown in the photo at left. (U.S. Navy)

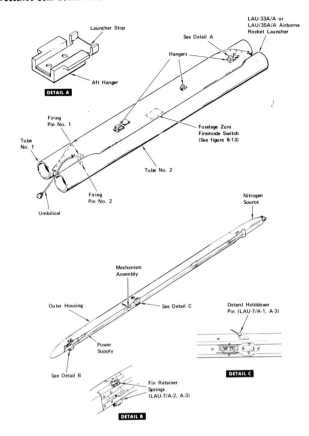

A double Zuni launcher is attached to the right fuselage station on an F-8H from VF-201. *(Flightleader)*

A double-barreled Zuni rocket launcher could be attached to the Sidewinder launch rails, thus increasing the ground attack capability of the Crusader. These launchers could be mounted to the single rail arrangement or the two rails used on the "Y" racks.

(U.S. Navy)

This Crusader is loaded with Zuni launchers on its "Y" racks and multiple ejector racks (MER) on its wing pylons. The combination of guns, rockets, and bombs made the Crusader a fairly effective fighter-bomber even though it was not originally intended for this mission.

(U.S. Navy)

This F-8E is also armed with Zunis on its "Y" racks and Mark 81 bombs on MERs attached to its wing pylons. Triple ejector racks could also be used to carry three bombs in the 750 pound class. *(U.S. Navy)*

Larger single bombs up to the 2000 pound variety could be attached to the wing pylons. *(U.S. Navy)*

"Y" racks to carry two Sidewinders on the fuselage stations replaced the earlier single mount. At left, the missiles are being checked on a VF-51 aircraft aboard the USS TICONDEROGA prior to a mission. At right is the "Y" rack on the left side of an F-8D. (Both U.S. Navy)

This Crusader is on the starboard cat on the USS TICONDEROGA, CVA-14, ready for a strike against Vietnam. Two Sidewinders are on single rails on the fuselage stations, and Zuni rocket pods are on the wing pylons. Each pod carries four rockets. (Flightleader)

Bullpup guided air-to-surface missiles could also be carried on the wing stations. The guidance equipment for the Bullpup missile was housed in the fairing on top of the fuselage and wing center section. (U.S. Navy)

This close-up provides a better look at bombs loaded on a MER that is attached to the right pylon. These are Mark 81 bombs. (U.S. Navy)

Rockeyes could also be loaded on the MERs. This photo shows Rockeyes being dropped from a Crusader during compatibility tests between the Crusader and the Rockeye. (U.S. Navy)

This F-8E has an AQM-37A drone mounted on its wing station. *(U.S. Navy)*

An F-8A from Utility Squadron 7 is beginning to reel out a target from its left wing prior to gunnery practice. *(U.S. Navy)*

Another type of target carried by the Crusader was the Aero 22-B, which is attached to an LAU-37A launcher carried under the left wing. Note that this is not the standard wing station. A 43M reel is mounted on the fuselage station, as it was with the target system shown in the center right photograph. *(U.S. Navy)*

This is a close-up of the Aero 22-B target on the LAU-37A launcher. *(U.S. Navy)*

APPROXIMATE GROUND CLEARANCES*

A — Wing tip (wing down) ....5 FEET 6 INCHES
            (wing up) ....3 FEET 6 INCHES
B — Duct lip ....3 FEET 9 INCHES
C — Tail cone ....2 FEET
D — Ventral fin ....1 FOOT 4 INCHES

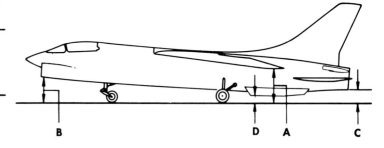

*Clearances vary slightly with aircraft loading and strut and tire servicing.

SERVICING POINTS

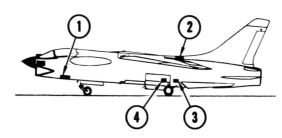

PC 2 Reservoir Indicator

1. Electrical power
2. Engine oil
3. Engine starter
4. Fuel system (central-point fueling)

5. Utility hydraulic system
6. Oxygen system
7. Pneumatic system
8. Tires

9. Power control hydraulic systems (PC 2 shown, PC 1 in same location in LH wheel well)
10. Generator constant speed drive (CSD)
11. Smoke abatement system

F8U-1P/RF-8A/RF-8G

Along with the fighter version, a reconnaissance Crusader was ordered in the form of the F8U-1P, which was later redesignated the RF-8A. The camera bays gave the lower forward fuselage a more boxy or squared cross-section than the fighters. A noticeable hump was added just behind the canopy to compensate for the enlarged lower fuselage in the aircraft's area rule design. This photograph shows an RF-8A from VFP-52 aboard the USS SARATOGA, CVA-60. (Flightleader)

Like all of the fighter versions except for the F-8A, RF-8As were part of a remanufacturing program that improved capabilities and extended the service life of the Crusader. This is an RF-8G, which was a remanufactured version of the RF-8A. Note the addition of the ventral strakes which are not present on the unmodified RF-8A at left. This photograph was taken aboard the USS JOHN F. KENNEDY, CV-67. (Flightleader)

F8U-1, 141363, was converted to the camera-carrying prototype for the F8U-1P, which was subsequently redesignated RF-8A. The first flight of a photo Crusader was made on December 17, 1956, and a total of 144 were built. In most respects the RF-8A was similar to the basic F-8A, except that the fuselage forward of the main wheel wells was redesigned to carry cameras instead of guns. This caused a noticeable flattening to the sides and bottom of the fuselage, and a hump behind the canopy that extended back on to the center section of the wing. This hump was necessary to maintain the proper area rule or "coking" of the fuselage. Five or six cameras could be carried, and at first, three trimetrogen and two vertical cameras were normally installed. Photo-flash cartridges could be carried internally for night photography. Electronic equipment carried in the RF-8A was as follows.

VHF Navigation Receiver AN/ARN-14E
UHF Transmitter/Receiver AN/ARC-21
UHF Direction Finder AN/ARA-25
IFF Transponder AN/APX-6B
Coder AN/APA-89
Radar Altimeter AN/APN-22

As originally built, the RF-8As did not have the ventral fins or the cooling scoops for the afterburner. Another difference was that the in-flight refueling probe was housed completely inside the fuselage rather than being in a blister as it was on the fighter versions. Like the F-8A, the RF-8A was powered by the J57-P-4 engine.

Captain George S. Morrison, the commanding officer aboard the USS BON HOMME RICHARD, CVA-31, signals the 50,000th accident-free catapult launch aboard that carrier. The date of this milestone was February 1, 1964, and it was accomplished by an RF-8A from VFP-63. (U.S. Navy)

An RF-8G from VFP-63 returns to the USS ORISKANY, CVA-34, after a mission. The RF-8G was a remanufactured RF-8A, and was the last dedicated photographic reconnaissance aircraft operated by the Navy.

(U.S. Navy)

In 1963, five RF-8As had their wings strengthened, and ventral fins were added under the aft fuselage. This led to the beginning of a remanufacturing program that resulted in the RF-8G. Fifty-three aircraft were upgraded between 1965 and 1967, and twenty more followed between 1968 and 1970, for a total of seventy-three airframes. Improvements included a stronger wing spar, ventral fins, additional navigation and electronic equipment, multi-position openings for the cameras, ECM equipment and the associated antennas, and fuselage reinforcement. Test pilot Joe Engle flew the first RF-8G on August 31, 1965. The last American Crusaders to fly were RF-8Gs assigned to VFP-206 at NAF Andrews, Maryland.

Like their fighting cousins, RF-8s were used extensively in Vietnam. All were assigned to VFP-63, based at NAS Miramar, and detached to various carriers for combat duty. Earlier, RF-8As had participated in flights over Cuba before and during the blockade in 1962, and John Glenn had used the RF-8A in his historic record-setting trans-continental flight as related in the Historical Summary portion of this book.

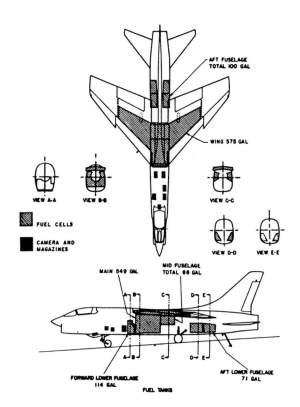

RF-8A PERFORMANCE CHARACTERISTICS

Take-off weight	27,822 lbs.
Fuel	10,176 lbs.
Payload	520 lbs.
Wing loading	74.2 lbs./sq. ft.
Stall speed-power off	137.2 kts.
T.O. run, S.L. (calm)*	5,600 ft.
T.O. run, S.L. (25 kt. wind)*	4,170 ft.
Max speed/altitude*	585/10,000 ft.
Rate of climb at S.L.*	5,050 fpm.
Service ceiling*	41,600 ft.
Combat range	1,740 n. mi.
Average cruising speed	495 kts.
Combat radius/mission time	640 n. mi./2.84 hr.

* Military thrust, no afterburner

These performance characteristics are for a standard aircraft flying a high altitude photo reconnaissance mission.

Source: U.S. Navy Standard Aircraft Characteristics

One of the differences between the recon versions and the fighter versions was that the retractable refueling probe was located inside the fuselage of the recon versions rather than being in a blister. At left is a view from the front, and at right is a close-up of the compartment. A color photograph of the entire probe, and a comparison to a fighter type probe, can be seen on page 36.

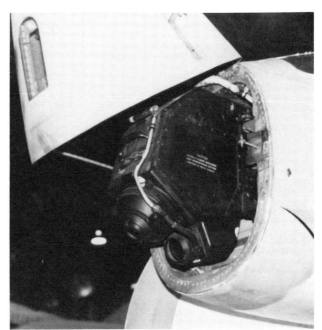

These two views show the camera mounted in the nose of an RF-8G.

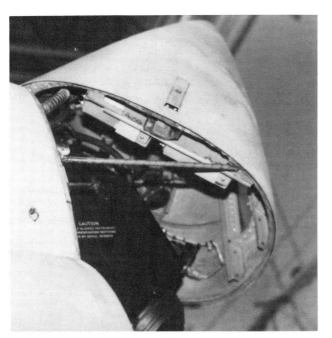
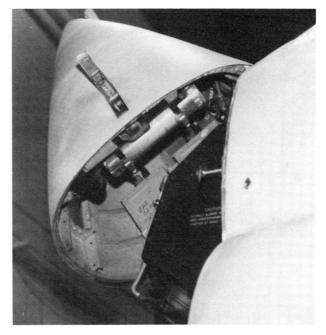

Center left and right: Details of the interior of the nose cone are seen in these two views.

Left: This front view of the nose cone shows the camera window to good effect.

Camera installations varied considerably throughout the years on the RF-8A and RF-8G aircraft. Different camera arrangements could be carried at any one time. At left is a forward-looking camera in a blister under an RF-8G. At right is an oblique camera location to the right of the nose gear well.

CAMERA BAY DETAILS

This photograph shows a camera installed in the vertical position on the right side of the aircraft. The camera can be rotated to take photographs to the side through the window in the door.

Two large windows for vertical cameras can be seen in this view.

This camera is installed in bay 3 of an RF-8G.

Photographer's mates are checking cameras in bays 2 and 3 in an RF-8G from VFP-306. (U.S. Navy)

Bays 2 and 3 are shown open on an early RF-8A. (U.S. Navy)

MODELERS SECTION
MODEL KITS

1/300th SCALE

Nichimo F-8E, Kit Number 24

This is the smallest F-8 Crusader model available, save for the aircraft that come as part of the air wings for aircraft carrier kits. It was released in 1984, and is packaged with an A-6E Intruder. It has very fine, engraved panel lines, and fit is quite good. Included are two underwing bombs and two Sidewinders for the fuselage. The model comes complete with a landing gear, or it can be built in a gear-up, in-flight configuration. The decal sheet is very complete with markings for VF-162 with a tail code AH. In fact, it is better than some sheets for larger scale models. However, fitting the decals on such small curved surfaces caused some problems. The normal thickness of the decals prevented them from adhering to these surfaces, and most had to be glued on.

1/144th SCALE

Otaki F-8C, Kit Number A3

Nineteen pieces in medium gray plastic make up this small model. All 1/144th scale kits of the F-8 released so far are re-releases of this basic kit and have the same problems. The strakes and gear doors should be replaced with thinner plastic card, and the afterburner cooling scoops should be added. The landing gear is very tricky to get level. Some basic cockpit detailing is needed, because the area is clearly visible under the canopy. Shapes and outlines are incorrect in a number of places. Most noticeably, the fairing for the in-flight refueling probe is way too large, as are the gun fairings. Another major problem is configuration for the Sidewinder missiles and their launch rails. Two single rails are provided for each side of the fuselage rather than "Y" rails, and the top rail is further aft than the lower one. This is backwards from the real thing, and appears to have been done so they would fit over the overly large blister for the refueling probe on the left side. The simplest solution is to use one

of the rails for each side in the single rail configuration. But sand that blister down to shape first. The intake lip needs to be thinned and reshaped.

Decals include two national insignias, two **NAVY**s, two **AJ** tail codes, two small **205**s, and two larger **205AJ**s. All are in the wrong shade of blue.

This is not one of the better kits in 1/144th scale, and much work would have to be done to get it to look right. Unfortunately, it is the only 1/144th scale kit available of the Crusader.

Comments by Jim Galloway

Entex F-8C, Kit Number 8461C

Entex re-released the Otaki kit with no major changes. The plastic is white, and the lettering on the decal sheet is black instead of blue. Otherwise the markings are the same. This kit is now worth between two and four dollars to collectors.

Arii F-8C, Kit Number A393

This is simply the Otaki kit released yet again in 1987. Even the decals are the same as in the Otaki kit. The plastic is light gray. Arii also included this in their multiple kit A381, which also contained an F-100, F-101, F-4, F-5, and MiG-23. Again it is identical to the Otaki release.

1/100th SCALE

Takara F-8E, Kit Number 441002-6

This is the only F-8 in 1/100th scale, and it is an excellent kit. It has finely engraved panel lines and control surfaces and is crisply molded. A total of forty-three parts are included in gray plastic plus a clear canopy. The cockpit only has a seat and a pilot figure, so most modelers will want to add some detailing. Fit is generally good, but the fuselage halves leave a bad seam inside the intake that is very hard to get rid of. Ordnance includes four Sidewinders, and four bombs of two different sizes for the

These two Otaki 1/144th scale Crusaders were built by Jim Galloway. The one on the left was built years ago, and has kit markings, while the one on the right was built recently and has Microscale decals. The missile mounts for this kit are totally incorrect.

The Takara 1/100th scale kit is quite good. This one was built by Jim Galloway and has markings for VF-191.

wing pylons. For the modeler who wants to build a diorama, there is a three man ground crew and two dollies for the bombs. The inside bottom of the box has a section of tarmac printed on it which can also be used in the diorama.

Decals are for a CAG aircraft from VF-191 and the USS Oriskany. Alternate decals are given for the fictitious Royal Aslan Air Force from a Japanese comic strip. On our review sample, the decals turned brittle shortly after application, so be sure to get your gloss coat, then a flatter finish, on them as soon as possible.

Hobbycraft F-8, Kit Number not known

Hobbycraft has announced the release of a Crusader in 1/100th scale, but it was not available at press time for this book. Whether it will be a re-release of the Takara kit or a new issue is not known at this time.

1/72nd SCALE

ACE F-8E, Kit Number 1200

The kit is molded in light gray plastic and features recessed panel lines. The first impression is that it is an improvement over the Hasegawa kit that has been around for quite a few years. However, closer inspection will reveal that not too much improvement has been made. The cockpit area is devoid of detail. The cockpit tub is a slab of plastic that consists of the floor, two rather nondescript side consoles, and a flat instrument panel. The seat comes in two pieces that leave a real bad seam. Detailing in the cockpit is provided only by three decals.

The windscreen is fairly thin and free of mold marks. It fits to the fuselage fairly well. The canopy is also pretty good, but is lacking the hinge tabs. This means that the only way to display it is in the closed position unless you want to do a lot of work.

The fuselage fits together fairly well, but there is a bad seam at the top of the rudder which has to be filled and sanded. The cannon ports should be drilled out, and this will greatly enhance their appearance. The intake is simply a hole with no ducting or closure panel. The easiest solution here is a scratchbuilt FOD cover. At the other end, the tail cone is made up of three pieces and two afterburner cooling scoops. The scoops are too large and round, although the length seems correct. The ventral fins are included but appear to be a little small. Cut off the locating pins and fill the grooves the fins are supposed to fit into. Then glue the fins to the fuselage in the proper location, and be ready for a lot of filling and sanding. The fit is terrible.

The landing gear does not look too bad, but replacing the main wheels with thicker ones will help. The nose gear is molded in one piece, so painting and detailing it out of the box will be difficult. A total rework of the nose gear is recommended. Detailing inside the gear wells is adequate, but can be enhanced greatly with a few wires, etc.

One of the newest 1/72nd scale kits is this model from ACE. It was built by Ed Hulsey.

The main wing is molded so that one can install the wing in a raised position if you also drop the droops, flaps, and ailerons. It is probably easier to do this instead of trying to get the wing to fit to the fuselage. Lots of cutting and reworking, not to mention filling and sanding, is required here.

External armament consists of two bombs for the wing pylons, and Sidewinders for the "Y" rails. On our review sample, the "Y" rails did not look that good, so they were replaced with single rails instead.

The decals are a real mystery. On the first sample kit they were washed out and not really defined. A second kit was obtained, and in it the printing for the decals was very heavy. The carrier film was thin, but stood up to rough handling and Solvaset like iron. The markings are for an F-8E, 150849, from VF-102. The tail code is **NF.**

Review by Ed Hulsey

Fujimi F-8D, Kit Number FG2

The Fujimi offering of the F-8 Crusader is one of the older F-8 kits, dating back to the mid-to-late 1960s. It is very dated by today's standards, and quite frankly, it is not that good by any standard. It is simply not acceptable for the scale modeler, and in no way compares favorably with the excellent kits Fujimi is releasing today. It consists of forty-six parts molded in light gray, and a clear canopy and windscreen. Fit of these parts is fair-to-good. Surface detail consists of hundreds of large, raised rivets that would be softball size or larger if scaled up to the size of the real thing. The panel lines are recessed. There are some outline problems and other inaccuracies, and the kit does not measure out to be a true 1/72nd scale.

The cockpit is crude, consisting of an instrument panel, crude pilot figure, and a shelf-like seat. Other drawbacks are an incorrect afterburner shape, incorrect afterburner cooling scoops, and missing gun bulges. The canopy is a one-piece affair and can only be displayed in the closed position. Even then it doesn't fit well. The two Sidewinder "Y" racks are fair, although they lack detail.

During assembly, the kit required very little filling but moderate sanding to remove the rivets. Although the

The old Fujimi F-8 is the worst of the 1/72nd scale models of the Crusader. It is not even in the same world as the excellent 1/72nd scale models that Fujimi has released recently. This one was built by Robert Starnes, a junior modeler and a member of IPMS Atlanta.

The Hasegawa model was used by Don Harris of Lawrenceville, Georgia, to build this Crusader in VF-191's CAG markings.

exploded view on the instruction sheet does not mention it, the wings can be raised into the take-off and landing position if you drop the droops, flaps, and ailerons.

The decal sheet includes markings for VF-111 and very basic Marine markings. They are of fair quality and adhesion is excellent. Some important stenciling and the colorful VF-111 tail sunburst markings are not included, but can be found on Microscale sheet 72-85.

Considering the $7.50 price and the availability of better F-8 kits in 1/72nd scale, this kit cannot be recommended for the serious modeler.

Review by Robert Starnes

Hasegawa F-8E, Kit Numbers JS146 and EO17:600

The modeler is given three sprue tree sections in gray plastic plus one clear sprue tree containing the canopy and windscreen. The parts are finely molded and very crisp with no flash and a minimum of mold release marks. Fit is excellent with very little filling and sanding required. Some of the detail is engraved, but the majority of the panel lines are raised. They are very petite.

Cockpit detailing is in the form of decals for the instrument panel and consoles. The seat is a two-piece affair which will require some work to fill the gap left once the two pieces are glued together. The control column needs to be reworked or replaced, having a "Y" shape to it that doesn't look much like the real thing. The model can be built with the refueling probe extended, and this is a nice touch, but an open speed brake would have also added a lot to the model. If you look down the intake you see the cockpit tub, so a FOD cover should be added unless you want to try to add ducting. If the kit is built right out of the box, viewing it from the front makes it look like a toy since the cockpit is clearly visible inside the intake. This is probably the major problem with the kit.

The main landing gear and wheels are nicely detailed, and the wheel wells show some basic (although inaccurate) plumbing and wiring. The nose wheel and strut are all one piece, and it would have been better if they had been made separately. The nose wheel well is too shallow

and is not detailed. The wing can be built in the raised position if the modeler is willing to drop the droops, flaps, and ailerons.

The kit provides the "Y" racks for four Sidewinder missiles and underwing pylons for two bombs, so the model can be built "loaded." The canopy parts are thin and quite clear. The tail cone alone is made of five pieces and is very representative of the real thing.

Kit decals are for two aircraft, one from VF-162 and the USS Oriskany, with a tail code of **AH,** and the second is a Marine Crusader from VMF (AW)-312. It has a tail code of **DR.** Our review sample was completed with Microscale decals for VF-191.

Overall this is an easy model to build, and, with a little work in the detailing department, will enhance anyone's collection. Fit is better than the new Revell and ACE kits which otherwise follow the lines of this model very closely.

Review by Don Harris

Heller F-8E (FN) and F-8E/-J, Kit Number 259

Molded in gray and clear plastic, this kit features optional (larger) horizontal stabilizers for building the French version of the Crusader as well as the F-8J. It also has panel lines representing the double hinged leading edge droops, and is therefore the best kit for building these two versions of the Crusader in 1/72nd scale. Clear parts consist of a canopy/windscreen, landing light, and two nose pieces for the Matra missiles. Fifty-one gray parts comprise the rest of the kit.

Although the panel lines are represented by very petite raised plastic, Heller got carried away with rivets. They are numerous and large. Other than these rivets, a canopy that is too thick, poor decals, and instructions that are almost useless, it is hard to fault this kit. It went together well, and very little filling and sanding was necessary. The lip of the intake and the trailing edges of the flying surfaces are exceptionally thin, and care should be taken during construction not to damage them.

The cockpit has very little in the way of detailing, so most modelers will want to take some time to add at least

Clyde Mills took the time to raise the wing and reposition the droops, ailerons, and flaps on the Heller 1/72nd scale model.

a minimum of details. There is some detailing inside the main gear wells, but there is nothing in the nose gear well.

Decals are provided for both American and French aircraft. VF-194 from the USS Ticonderoga and VF-24 from the USS Hancock are the American units that are represented, while both French Navy squadrons are represented. These appear to be yellowed and brittle, so Microscale markings were used on the review sample representing VMF (AW)-122.

Review by Clyde Mills

Minicraft F-8E, Kit Number JS146

This is the Minicraft release of the Hasegawa 1/72nd scale kit reviewed above. It is identical in all respects except for the box art and decals which represent an aircraft from VF-111 and the USS Shangri-La.

Revell F-8, Kit Numbers H250, H154, H167, H295, H255

The original Revell Crusader model was released a number of times as indicated above. The first release, H250, was in 1956, followed by H154 in 1960, H167 in 1961, H295 in 1963, and H255 in 1967. All are now considered collector's items. Although basically the same kit, Revell did make some updates to include the addition of "Y" racks and ventral fins beginning with H167. It was not actually 1/72nd scale, measuring closer to 1/67th scale instead. A brief summary of each kit is followed below by a complete review of H255.

H250 was the original issue and represented an F8U-1. It came with a three-piece clear swivel stand and had fictitious markings, representing no particular unit. This kit now brings from twelve to seventeen dollars from collectors. No changes were made in H154 except that the stand was deleted in favor of a string and clay weight so that you could "whip fly" the model. A metal ring was attached through a hole in the left wing, and a ten-foot long string was tied to the ring. A rather complex formula was on the instruction sheet to allow the kids to figure

miles per hour, but no landing instructions were provided. Usually the landing gear would be wiped out on the first landing! Someone else can figure the kinetic energy of a one-pound model at the end of a ten-foot string making two complete revolutions a second! Decals provided only the basic national insignia and three **NAVY**s. It is worth between eight and twelve dollars to collectors.

Kit H167 was in the famous artist series, and it contained the updates of ventral fins and "Y" racks mentioned above. Decals were the factory markings used on the F8U-2N prototype. Its present market value for collectors ranges between eight and twelve dollars. Kit H295 was essentially the same, but we have no further information on it other than the fact that it brings between five and nine dollars from collectors.

Kit H255 is the most recent release of this Revell model, but is still an adult, being over twenty-one years old. A sample of this kit was built for this book, and a review follows.

This kit is in Revell's "Jet Commando" series, and is an update of the earlier F8U-1. In its day it was considered an outstanding kit, but today it takes a lot of work to bring it up to the standards of a present out-of-the-box model. However, if the modeler is willing to do the work, an attractive model of the Crusader can be constructed.

To represent an F-8E, Revell added the larger radome, but it is oversized and should be made smaller. The "Y" racks for the Sidewinders and four "usable" missiles are included, as are two grossly inaccurate ventral fins. These are easily replaced by the modeler from plastic card. Missing are the IR sensor, the dorsal avionics pack, the afterburner cooling scoops, and the underwing pylons with stores.

The blister for the refueling probe is molded at an odd angle to the fuselage, and is the wrong size and shape. It is best removed and replaced with a new one made from plasic card. The fairings for the cannons are too small and

The old Revell kit was released several times, both as an F-8A and a later F-8C and F-8E. This release, H-255, was built by Jim Whitley. It is a good kit considering that it was first released in the 1950s, but it not as good as the later, more up-to-date kits.

are plugged as they were on the prototypes. Other surface detail consists of very petite raised rivets, which are inappropriate for this airplane, and finely engraved panel lines which do not accurately represent those on the real aircraft.

Cockpit detailing consists solely of a pilot figure that is molded to a seat. This part is suspended from a peg on the inside of the fuselage. There are no consoles, floor, instrument panel, stick, or bulkhead. In short, an entire cockpit must be built. The canopy is poorly done, and a new one should be vacu-formed.

There are some shape and outline problems. In addition to the oversized radome, the nose profile is too shallow due to the incorrect flat bottom of the intake which should be more oval. There is a baffle in the intake which eliminates the "see-through" effect, but it would look nicer with a FOD cover in place. The aft fuselage is too tapered, the tail pipe is too long, and the exhaust is too small. The afterburner flameholder is molded at the end of the pipe, and a better appearance can be obtained by cutting it out and mounting it inside the fuselage. This will open up the pipe and give it more depth. The vertical tail sweeps back a bit too much, and its trailing edge is a little too far aft.

The wing can be built in the folded or extended position and appears correct in planform except that the wing-fold hinge line and dog tooth on the leading edge are slightly too far outboard. The span is correct. The folding mechanism is toy-like, and not at all like the real thing. Since the wing roots plug into the fuselage, modeling it in the raised position would require major surgery.

The landing gear is poorly done, and it might be best to consider a gear-up configuration. Decals are for an F-8E, 149172, from VF-111. The tail code is **AB,** and the modex is **211.**

Review by Jim Whitley

Revell F-8E, Kit Number 4364

This kit is not to be confused to the earlier Revell releases. It is a completely new kit in 1/72nd scale, and was released in 1988, just a few months before the release of this book. It is molded by Revell in Korea, and, comparing it with the Hasegawa (Japan) and ACE (Korea) kits, it appears to be a copy of a copy. At first glance in the box it appears to be a very nice kit. Outlines, shapes, and dimensions are quite good. There are the typical Revell picture instructions, and the decals are glossy but usable. Panel lines are the recessed type. The reason it appears to be a copy of the ACE kit is that all panels match, including some rivets that are not straight. But there are differences as well. The outboard wing panels are separate pieces, the vertical tail is separate from the fuselage, and the seat is a single piece rather than being split vertically. It lacks detail.

There are two points where this model suffers. The first is detailing, and the second is fit. The cockpit has the basic floor and consoles with no detailing. The instru-

Ray Wheeler built this model using the new Revell 1/72nd scale kit.

ment panel is the wrong shape, is flat, and is located too far back. The control stick looks like a divining rod, and there is no gunsight. When you look into the intake you have a nice view of the bottom of the cockpit. This would be all right if a FOD cover was included in the kit to cover the intake, but it would have been better yet if the ducting for the intake was supplied. There is some "busy" detailing in the main gear wells, but the nose gear well isn't even large enough to accommodate the gear. The main gear is good except that the wheels are too thin and should be replaced. The nose wheel and strut are all one piece, and this makes it a lot of fun to paint. The afterburner can looks good except that the cooling scoops appear to be too tall and too rounded.

Poor fit makes building this model a nightmare. The cockpit tub is too wide for the fuselage halves, so it must be trimmed to fit. The wings are not square in relation to the slot that they "fit" into. If the wing is built in the lowered position, getting it to fit and filling the seams and gaps is a monumental task. There is another bad fit problem if the outboard wing panels are attached in the extended position. So much filling and sanding is required that all surface detailing is removed. The hinge line on the bottom isn't even close. It would scale out to be the size of a 6 x 6 board.

The most difficult parts to make look right were the ventral fins. It is best to cut off the locating pins since they don't fit in the holes anyway. Glue the fins to the model, then get out the sandpaper and filler!

The clear pieces are correct in shape, but again the fit is bad. The windscreen does not mate to the fuselage. The canopy was evidently intended to be built in the closed position, since it is missing the hinges necessary to leave it open. However, it won't fit on the fuselage since it is too wide for the rails.

The armament consists of two bombs for the underwing pylons and four Sidewinders. The fins on the missiles are way too thick, and the forward fins are the wrong shape. These should be replaced. The "Y" racks for the missiles look quite good.

Decals are for an F-8E from VF-24 and the USS Hancock. The tail code is **NP.** Decals in our sample kits were quite out of register, particularly the white and yellow. This may not be a problem in all kits.

With the basic shapes being correct, this can be made

into a decent model of the Crusader if the modeler is up to solving all of the monumental fit problems.

Review by Ray Wheeler

Future F-8 kits from ERTL

At the 1988 Hobby Industry of American show in St. Louis, the ERTL company announced a new 1/72nd scale model of the Crusader. Their catalog showed at least two different issues of the kit. At press time for this book the model had not been released, so comments cannot be made about it.

Miscellaneous Vacuformed Kits in 1/72nd Scale

A number of companies have released vacuformed kits of the Crusader in 1/72nd scale. For the most part they are very hard to find, and are collector's items. One of the most interesting is an F8U-3 Crusader III from Hobby Import. The reason that this kit would hold interest over the others is that there is no injection-molded kit of this aircraft. Frank Modellbau, Fallon, and Airmodel have also offered kits of the Crusader in 1/72nd scale. The Airmodel kit is covered below under conversion kits since it can be used to build an RF-8.

1/48th SCALE

Aurora F8U, Kit Number 119

Having been released in 1957, this is one of the oldest models of the Crusader, and was based on the prototypes. It is in 1/50th scale rather than being a true 1/48th scale model. As with many kits from the 1950s, it is very "gimmicky," having retractable landing gear and a removable tail cone. It consists of forty-five pieces in light gray plastic plus a clear stand and canopy. The plastic is very hard and brittle, and it features football sized rivets and deep panel lines. Decals consist of four national insignias, a sharkmouth, three **NAVY**s, a red arrow for the fuselage side, and two yellow lightning flashes. There is no unit insignia.

This kit is a collector's item now, bringing eight to twelve dollars. It is not a kit for the serious modeler to build.

ESCI F-8E, Kit Number SC4011

Some of ESCI's early kits had some real fit problems, but this model of the F-8 Crusader appears to be one of the better ones. Fit is generally good throughout. The problem seems to be with warping in the wings, which was found on a good many of their kits that were released at about the same time of this 1981 offering. The amount of warping of the wings seems to vary from kit to kit, and can range from no warping at all to bends that are impossible to remove. One way to solve the problem is to cut the wing sections apart and build the wing in the folded position with the droops, flaps, and ailerons lowered. This means you are working with smaller pieces that are

A great deal of time and effort went into this model built by W. B. Baldwin. The ESCI 1/48th scale kit was used, and all squadron markings were hand painted.

easier to straighten than the entire wing assembly. W. B. Baldwin followed this procedure in building the model that is pictured with this review.

Seventy pieces in dark gray plastic comprise the bulk of the kit. The canopy, windscreen, and gunsight glass are provided in clear plastic. Panel lines are raised and are very fine. There is good detailing in the main gear wells and on the landing gear itself. The cockpit leaves a bit to be desired in the detailing department for such a large model. Decals are provided for the flat instrument panel and consoles. A little detailing here will go a long way to enhance the appearance of the model, particularly if the canopy is shown in the open position.

French markings are provided on the decal sheet, as are markings for VF-162 and VMF (AW)-312. The carrier name Oriskany is misspelled **ORYSKANY** for the aircraft from VF-162.

This is one of ESCI's better kits, and is worth building if you can find one without too much wing warping. It was clearly the best of the quarter scale Crusaders prior to the release of the Monogram kit.

Lindberg F8U, Kit Numbers 548 and 307M

Originally released in 1960, this kit is loaded with working features. It has movable flaps, ailerons, rudder, and stabilizers. The ejection seat "ejects," and the landing gear retracts. The aft section of the fuselage can be removed to reveal the engine, and 307M even had an electric motor to produce an engine sound. There are fifty-five pieces in white plastic, a four-piece silver stand, and a two-piece clear canopy. Decals are only the basics, consisting of national insignia and three **NAVY**s. This is a collector's item, so collect it and forget it--don't build it! The original issue, 548, goes for about three to six dollars, while the motorized 307M is now worth from six to ten dollars.

Monogram F-8E, New Release

At the 1988 Hobby Industry of America show, Monogram announced the release of a 1/48th scale F-8 Cru-

The new Monogram kit promises to be the best Crusader model in any scale. This publicity photograph from Monogram reveals some of the kit's features. (Monogram)

sader for late in the year. That release had not been made at the press time for this book, but Monogram was kind enough to provide Detail & Scale with a test shot of the kit. The test shot was an early one without any of the surface scribing, so we cannot comment on that. Based on recent Monogram releases, we expect that it will be quite good. It is also not a true test to judge the fit of a final kit based on a test shot, so we are unable to make any statements about the fit of the model. As would be expected, the test shot has no decals, no box, and no instructions. What we can say is that it looks like this will be far and away the best Crusader in any scale. We are very anxious to see the final product.

Cockpit detailing is accurate, complete, and finely done. However, the ejection seat is not correct. Once the final scribing is on the instrument panel and consoles, they will demand care and patience in painting to bring out their details. A typical Monogram pilot figure is provided, but it would only cover some of the beautiful detailing in the cockpit. The control column is nicely done, and looks like the real thing. A gunsight glass in clear plastic rounds out the cockpit detailing. To keep the cockpit from being visible inside of the intake, Monogram has supplied ducting to fit in the intake. A detailed and complete nose gear well fits under the ducting.

The landing gear is equally well detailed. On the inside brace for the nose gear (part 25) even the lightening holes are molded in. The nose gear strut and wheel are separate pieces that add a lot to the model and ease to the construction and painting. The main landing gear is equally as nice, and there is a good deal of detailing in the wells. The refueling probe can be shown in the closed or extended position.

"Y" racks are provided for four Sidewinder missiles on the fuselage stations, while wing pylons with triple ejector racks and bombs are supplied for the wing stations. Very small holes are in the lower wings for locating the pylons, so if you don't want to use them, they are easily deleted. The wings are a top-bottom design for the center sections, while the outer sections are separate and each one-piece. The wing attaches to an open area in the top of the fuselage, so the only way to build the wing in the raised position will be to scratchbuild the entire inside of the area under the center section of the wing. It is for this

reason that we included the photographs on page 51.

The windscreen, canopy, landing light, and gunsight glass are all represented in thin clear plastic. The canopy has the appropriate hinges, so showing it in the open position will be easy. All in all this looks like another winner from Monogram, and it should be a very popular kit.

1/32nd SCALE

Combat Models, Kit Number 30

The largest kit presently available of the Crusader is a vacuformed model from Combat Models in 1/32nd scale. Two large white sheets contain all of the plastic parts to include fuselage halves, engine halves, wings, intake interior, seat, main landing gear wheels and doors, and four Sidewinder missiles. A third flat sheet of plastic stock is also provided from which other parts can be made. The landing gear struts and nose wheel are supplied as metal parts. A clear, single-piece canopy/windscreen combination rounds out the kit's parts. A decal sheet is also provided, and contains basic U.S. Army, Navy, and Marine markings.

As with most vacuformed kits, there is a lot of work for the modeler to do, and some shape problems to correct. Most noticeable is the blister for the in-flight refueling probe which is too large and is at the wrong angle. The radome, wing tips, and the tip of the vertical tail will also require some work, but anyone with the skills to build this kit will have little trouble correcting these. The outer wing panels are separate from the center section, so a model with the wings in the folded position is the easiest option. The horizontal stabilizers and ventral fins have to be cut from stock plastic.

The instruction sheet shows four full views and one scrap view, but the written instructions are generic for vacuformed kits rather than being specifically for the Crusader. Most large vacuformed kits require a considerable amount of skill on the part of the modeler, knowledge of the subject, and innovation when it comes to detailing and building the model. This kit is no exception,

The 1/32nd scale vacuformed kit from Combat Models is the largest Crusader model available. This is a display model built by the manufacturer, and it was photographed at the 1988 IPMS National Convention.

but with patience, persistence, and time, this kit could be built into a good model of the Crusader. Unless a kit manufacturer produces an injected model of a Crusader in 1/32nd scale, and that is highly unlikely, this is the best place to start. The only other alternative is to build from scratch.

Information about ordering this kit can be obtained by writing to Combat Models, 400 Third Street, West Easton, PA 18042. Send seventy-five cents for their most recent price list and a SASE with your inquiry.

CONVERSION KITS

Airmodel RF-8, Kit Number 323

Although this was marketed as a complete 1/72nd scale vacuformed kit rather than a conversion kit, it supplies only the fuselage and wings. Everything else must be scratchbuilt or scrounged from the parts box. The wing does not have the proper hump for the RF-8, and the fuselage lacks detail. There are some major shape problems. We cannot recommend this kit.

Falcon/War Eagle Triple Conversion Kit

This vacuformed kit provides parts for the F-100F, TA-7C, and RF-8G in 1/72nd scale. For the Crusader, the fuselage from the main wheel wells forward is provided, as is the top of the wing center section with the RF-8 hump. There is no scribing or detailing on the fuselage to speak of, and only the droops are on the wing. The parts are molded better than the Airmodel kit. We think that it would have been better if the entire fuselage had been provided. Having a forward fuselage that is vacuformed with no detailing and an aft fuselage that is injected molded can cause some problems. But the wing may be even harder to work with. Only the top part of the center section is included, so you have to mate this to a lower center section and the outboard panels. The fit, particularly to the outer panels, is bound to cause some problems, and will require a lot of filling and sanding. An alternative might be to cut the hump from the vacuformed wing and mate it to the complete injected wing in the Hasegawa kit. This would also take some filling and sanding, but it would be in a less critical area than at the wing fold.

The instructions are very incomplete and say nothing about the assembly of the wing. The drawings show only the front view of an RF-8, and contribute nothing to the assembly of the model.

Nose Job White Metal Conversion Kit

This conversion "kit" provides two smaller nose radomes in white metal to convert the 1/72nd scale Hasegawa/ACE/Revell to an F-8A or F-8B. The instructions show how to fit the new nose, and explain that the avionics hump has to be removed and filled. It does not explain that the ventral fins and afterburner cooling scoops must be removed, and a saber drain must be added.

War Eagle RF-8 Conversion Kit

This is one of the best conversion kits we have ever seen. It is very well done and is designed to work with the ESCI kit in 1/48th scale. There are twelve vacuformed parts and a five-piece white metal ejection seat. Even high quality Scalemaster decals are provided for an RF-8G, 145613, from VFP-63 and the USS Franklin D. Roosevelt. The tail code is **AE,** and the modex is **601.** A second set of markings is provided for RF-8G, 146855, from VFP-306. The tail code is a stylized **ND,** and the modex is **602.** Black decals are supplied for the camera windows.

Keep in mind that this kit was designed to be used with the ESCI model in 1/48th scale. We believe that it could be built up into an outstanding model. How it would work with the new Monogram model we don't know, but we would expect that it would work better with the kit it was originally designed for. Regardless, it is obvious that the folks at War Eagle cared about their product, and made every attempt to make it a good one.

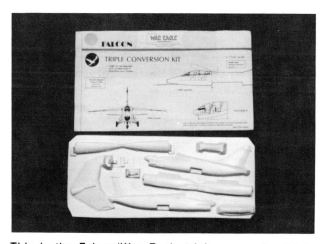

This is the Falcon/War Eagle triple conversion kit in 1/72nd scale. It includes parts to build an RF-8 Crusader.

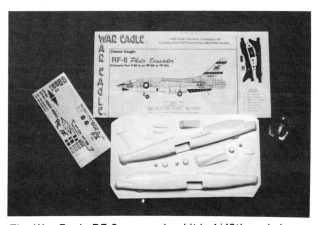

The War Eagle RF-8 conversion kit in 1/48th scale is one of the best and most complete conversion kits on the market. It even includes Scalemaster decals for two aircraft.

DECAL LISTING

Manufacturer and Sheet Number	Scale	Type	BuNo	Unit	Tail Code	Modex or Tail No.	Comments
ESCI 26	1/72nd	F-8E	149172	VF-11	AB	211	
		F-8C	146991	VF-111	AH	124	USS Oriskany
		F-8C	145559	VF-84	AG	200	USS Independence, CAG aircraft, Misidentified as an F-8E on the instruction sheet, and title is switched with VF-111 aircraft
		F-8A	143812	VMF-122	DC	16	Misidentified as an F-8E on the instruction sheet
Microscale 144-85*	1/144th	F-8C	146994	VF-24	NP	449	USS Hancock, BuNo indicates an F-8C, but instructions and decals misidentify this as an F-8E
		F-8H	148684	VF-111	AJ	105	USS Shangri-La
		F-8E	149203	VF-162	AH	200	USS Oriskany. This is an F-8E, but both decal and instruction sheet misidentify it as an F-8H
Microscale 144-86*	1/144th	F-8E	150318	VMF (AW)-235	DB	19	
		F-8C	145559	VMF (AW)-334	WU	12	
		F-8D	148639	VMF (AW)-333	DN	14	
		F-8E	150871	VMF (AW)-232	WT		
Microscale 144-204*	1/144th	F-8D	147062	VMF (AW)-451	VM	4	Misidentified on instruction sheet as an F-8E
		F-8K	145557	VMF-321	MG	11	
		F-8E	150675	VMF (AW)-312	DR	00	
Microscale 72-85	1/72nd	This sheet contains the same markings as Microscale sheet 144-85.					
Microscale 72-86	1/72nd	This sheet contains the same markings as Microscale sheet 144-86.					
Microscale 72-204	1/72nd	This sheet contains the same markings as Microscale sheet 144-204.					
Microscale 72-205	1/72nd	F-8J	149201	VF-24	NP	200	USS Hancock, CAG aircraft
		F-8C	145575	VF-84	AG	207	
Microscale 72-246	1/72nd	F-8E	150844	VF-13	AK	111	USS Shangri-La
		F-8E	149199	VF-211	NP	100	USS Hancock, CAG aircraft
		F-8J	150864	VF-194	NM	200	USS Oriskany, CAG aircraft
Microscale 72-301	1/72nd	F-8A	143705	VF-32	AC	202	USS Saratoga during crisis in Lebanon, 1958
Microscale 72-318	1/72nd	F-8E	149189	VF-51	NF	104	USS Hancock
Microscale 72-331	1/72nd	F-8E	149170	VF-33	AF	201	
Microscale 72-493	1/72nd	F-8A	143744	VF-142	NK	108	
Microscale 72-506	1/72nd	This sheet contains basic data and stencils for the F-8 Crusader.					
Microscale 48-82	1/48th	Contains markings for F-8E, 150318, and F-8C, 145559, as on sheet 144-86.					
Microscale 48-83	1/48th	Contains markings for F-8C, 146996, and F-8H, 148684, as on sheet 144-85.					
Microscale 48-211	1/48th	Contains markings for F-8C, 145575, as on sheet 72-205.					
Microscale 48-212	1/48th	F-8E	149199	VF-211	NP	100	USS Hancock, CAG aircraft
		F-8J	149201	VF-24	NP	200	USS Hancock, CAG aircraft
Microscale 48-222	1/48th	F-8E	150844	VF-13	AK	111	USS Shangri-La
		F-8J	150864	VF-194	NM	200	USS Oriskany, CAG aircraft
Microscale 48-266	1/48th	Contains markings for F-8D, 147062, and F-8K, 145557, as on sheet 144-204.					
Microscale 48-273	1/48th	Contains markings for F-8A, 143744, as on sheet 72-493.					
Microscale 48-282	1/48th	F-8E	150871	VMF (AW)-232	WT	2	
		F-8E	150675	VMF (AW)-321	DR	00	
Microscale 48-283	1/48th	This sheet contains basic data and stencils for the F-8 Crusader.					

* It should be noted that all of Microscale's 1/144th scale sheets are simply their 1/72nd scale sheets that are reproduced at one-half the 1/72nd scale size without regard to fit on the model. Therefore, fit in most cases is very bad.

This listing is current as of August 1988, which was the press time for this book. With new 1/72nd scale kits from Revell, ACE, and ERTL, and with the new 1/48th scale Crusader being released by Monogram, it can be expected that more new decal sheets will be forthcoming.